1A

A Communicative Course in English

Diane Warshawsky
with Donald R. H. Byrd

Donald R. H. Byrd *Project Director*

Anna Veltfort *Art Director*

PRENTICE HALL REGENTS
Englewood Cliffs, NJ 07632

Library of Congress has cataloged the full edition of this title as follows:

Warshawsky, Diane.
    Spectrum 1, a communicative course in English / Diane Warshawsky
with Donald R.H. Byrd; Donald R. H. Byrd, project director; Anna
Veltfort, art director.
        p   cm.
Also published in a two book split edition
ISBN 0-13-829862-9
    1. English language--Textbooks for foreign speakers.   I. Byrd,
Donald R.H.   II. Title.
PE1128.W36 1992
    428.2'4--dc20
                                                            91- 40867
                                                                CIP

ISBN (1A) 0-13-829870-X   ISBN (1B) 0-13-829888-2

Editorial Project Director: Deborah Goldblatt

Development Editor: Deborah Brennan
Contributing Editors: Larry Anger and Jeffrey Krum
Audio Editor: Stephanie Karras
Production Editor: Shari Toron
Pre-Press Buyer: Ray Keating
Manufacturing Buyer: Lori Bulwin
Scheduler: Leslie Coward
Cover Design: Roberto de Vicq
Interior and Page-by-Page Design: Anna Veltfort
Composition: Lisa Schneck
Audio Program Production: Phyllis Dolgin
Publisher: Tina B. Carver
Manager of Product Development: Mary Vaughn

©1992 by Prentice Hall Regents
Prentice-Hall, Inc.
A Simon & Schuster Company
Englewood Cliffs, New Jersey 07632

Printed in the United States of America

10

ISBN 0-13-829870-X

Prentice Hall International (UK) Limited, *London*
Prentice Hall of Australia Pty. Limited, *Sydney*
Prentice Hall Canada Inc., *Toronto*
Prentice Hall Hispanoamericana, S.A., *Mexico*
Prentice Hall of India Private Limited, *New Delhi*
Prentice Hall of Japan, Inc., *Tokyo*
Simon & Schuster Asia Pte. Ltd., *Singapore*
Editora Prentice Hall do Brasil, Ltda., *Rio de Janeiro*

I N T R O D U C T I O N

Spectrum 1A and 1B represent the first level of a six-level course designed for adolescent and adult learners of English. The student book, workbook, and audio program for each level provide practice in all four communication skills, with a special focus on listening and speaking. Levels 1 and 2 are appropriate for beginning students and "false" beginners. Levels 3 and 4 are intended for intermediate classes, and 5 and 6 for advanced learners of English. The first four levels are offered in split editions—1A, 1B, 2A, 2B, 3A, 3B, 4A, and 4B. The student books and workbooks for levels 1 to 4 are also available in full editions.

Spectrum is a "communicative" course in English, based on the idea that communication is not merely an end-product of language study, but rather the very process through which a new language is acquired. *Spectrum* involves students in this process from the very beginning by providing them with useful, natural English along with opportunities to discuss topics of personal interest and to communicate their own thoughts, feelings, and ideas.

In *Spectrum*, understanding a new language is considered the starting point for communication. The student books thus emphasize the importance of comprehension, both as a useful skill and as a natural means of acquiring a language. Students begin each unit by listening to and reading conversations that provide rich input for language learning. Accompanying activities enhance comprehension and give students time to absorb new vocabulary and structures. Throughout the unit students encounter readings and dialogues containing structures and expressions not formally introduced until later units or levels. The goal is to provide students with a continuous stream of input that challenges their current knowledge of English, thereby allowing them to progress naturally to a higher level of competence.

Spectrum emphasizes interaction as another vital step in language acquisition. Interaction begins with simple communication tasks that motivate students to use the same structure a number of times as they exchange real information about themselves and other topics. This focused practice builds confidence and fluency and prepares students for more open-ended activities involving role playing, discussion, and problem solving. These activities give students control of the interaction and enable them to develop strategies for expressing themselves and negotiating meaning in an English-speaking environment.

The *Spectrum* syllabus is organized around functions and structures practiced in thematic lessons. Both functions and structures are carefully graded according to simplicity and usefulness. Structures are presented in clear paradigms with informative usage notes. Thematic lessons provide interesting topics for interaction and a meaningful vehicle for introducing vocabulary.

Student Book 1A consists of seven units, each divided into one- and two-page lessons. The first lesson in each unit presents a series of authentic conversations, providing input for comprehension and language acquisition. A preview activity prepares students to understand the cultural material in the conversations. New functions and structures are then practiced through interactive tasks in several thematic lessons. A two-page, fully illustrated comprehension lesson provides further input in the form of a dialogue, pronunciation activity, and listening exercise all related to the storyline for the level. This lesson includes a role-playing activity as well. The final lesson of the unit presents authentic documents such as advertisements and news articles for reading comprehension practice. Review lessons follow units 1 to 4 and units 5 to 7.

Workbook 1A is carefully coordinated with the student book. Workbook lessons provide listening and writing practice on the functions, structures, and vocabulary introduced in the corresponding student book lessons. Units end with a guided composition related to the theme of the reading in the student book.

Audio Program 1A offers two cassettes for the student book with all conversations, model dialogues, listening activities, and readings dramatized by professional actors in realistic recordings with music and sound effects. A third cassette includes the workbook listening activities.

Teacher's Edition 1A features full-sized reproductions of each student-book page with teaching suggestions, listening scripts, and answer keys on the facing page. Listening scripts and answer keys for the workbook appear in the appendix.

A Testing Package includes a placement test as well as midterm and final tests for each level.

UNIT	PAGES	THEMES	FUNCTIONS
1 Lessons 1–7	A1–10	Greetings Introductions Self-identification	Introduce yourself Identify people Greet formally and informally Verify spelling
2 Lessons 8–13	A11–20	Telephone calls	Make an informal telephone call Identify someone on the telephone Ask for someone's phone number Call Directory Assistance Thank someone Ask for change Apologize
3 Lessons 14–19	A21–30	Cities and countries Socializing Addresses	Ask about the location of cities Ask where people are from Introduce people Offer something to drink Say good-bye after meeting someone Ask for someone's address
4 Lessons 20–25	A31–40	Neighborhood locations Directions	Give locations in a neighborhood Give locations in an apartment building Give directions in a neighborhood
Review of units 1–4	A41–44	Review	Review

S E Q U E N C E

LANGUAGE	FORMS	SKILLS

Hello. Hi. I'm Kenji Sato.
  My name is William Stone.
  Nice to meet you.
Excuse me, are you Tom Cruise?
  Yes, I am. No, I'm not.
How are you? Fine. Not bad.
What's your name, please?
  Could you spell your last name?
  N-I-E-L-S-E-N? Yes, that's right.
	Present of *be*:
	• *am, is*
	• contractions
	• questions with *are*
	• short answers with *I*
	Alphabet
	Formula *Could you . . . ?*
		Listen for a spelling
		Listen to the intonation of short
		  statements
		Read a postcard
		Write a short postcard to a friend
		  (workbook)

Is Susan there? Yes, she is. Just a minute,
  please. No, she isn't.
Is this Bill? No, this is Carlos.
What's your phone number? It's 555-2012.
I'd like the number of Jane Schaeffer.
Thank you. You're welcome.
Do you have change for a dollar?
Yes, I do. Here you are. No, I don't.
I'm sorry. That's O.K.
	Present of *be*:
	• yes-no questions and
	  short answers with *is*
	Numbers 0–10.
	Formula *I'd like . . .*
	Formulaic use of *do*
		Listen for a phone number
		Listen to the intonation of
		  questions
		Read a short newspaper article
		Write an opinion about the
		  telephone (workbook)

Where's Tokyo? In Japan.
Where are you from? I'm from Brazil.
The Lopezes are from Mexico.
Tony, this is my friend Linda.
  Linda, this is Tony.
Do you want some coffee? Yes, please.
  No, thank you.
Good-bye. Nice meeting you.
What's Jim's address? It's 60 Bank Street.
	Present of *be*:
	• information questions
	• statements
	• yes-no questions
	• short answers
	Plural of names
	Formulaic use of *do*
	Numbers 11–100
	Possessive of names
		Listen for addresses
		Listen to a radio advertisement
		Listen to the intonation of
		  statements and questions
		Read a letter and an envelope
		Write a short friendly letter
		  (workbook)

Is the post office near here? Where's
  the post office, please? On Second Avenue./
  Between Main and High Streets./Across
  from the park./Next to the restaurant./On
  the corner of Second and High.
Where's the Brunis' apartment? On the
  first floor.
Walk to the corner. Go straight ahead for
  two blocks. Turn right/left.
	Prepositions of place
	Ordinal numbers 1st–10th
	Possessive of names
	Imperative
	Adverbs of location
		Listen for directions
		Listen to the pronunciation of
		  possessives of names
		Read a page from a tour guide
		Write directions for a walking tour
		  (workbook)

Review	Review	Review

LANGUAGE	FORMS	SKILLS
Laura is an accountant. She works in an office. Accountants work in offices. What do you do? I'm a doctor. Where do you work? I work at Memorial Hospital. Do you live around here? Do you live in a house/an apartment? Where do you live? On Maple Street./At 25 Maple Street./ On the second floor./In apartment 2B. Are you married? No, I'm single.	Formulaic use of third person simple present in statements Articles *a* and *an* Plurals of nouns Simple present with *you* and *I*: • statements • questions • short answers Prepositions *in, on* and *at*	Listen for information about people Listen to consonant reduction and blending in *do you*, *is he*, and *is she* Read a short newspaper article on jobs Write about your job (workbook)
What's the date next Sunday? When's your birthday? It's February twelfth (12th). What year were you born? In 1971. Christine lives at 27 Willow Street. She goes to high school and she works at Macy's. Samuel and Nancy are husband and wife. Do you have any brothers or sisters? What does your sister do? What language do they speak in Jamaica? Do you speak Portuguese? Are you Brazilian? What does *mucho gusto* mean? How do you say "thank you" in Korean? Excuse me? Could you speak a little slower, please? Could I use your pencil? Sure. Here.	Ordinal numbers 11th–31st Formulaic use of *was* and *were* with *born* Simple present: • affirmative statements • irregular verbs • third person singular pronunciation • questions • negative statements • short answers Formula *Could I . . . ?* Terminology for family relationships	Listen for dates Listen to consonant reduction and blending in *What does he/she . . . ?* Read an advertisement Write a short paragraph about yourself (workbook)
May I help you? May I speak to Richard Lightner, please? May I take a message? Could you ask him to call me? I'll give him the message. Good morning/afternoon/evening. Good-bye./Good night./Have a nice weekend./See you tomorrow. What are you going to do this weekend? I'm going to visit a friend. What is Rob going to do this evening/ tomorrow night/next weekend/on Sunday?	Formula *May I . . . ?* Formula *I'll . . .* Object pronouns Formulaic use of future with *going to* Expressions of future time	Listen for names, days, and telephone numbers in phone conversations Listen for consonant reduction with pronouns *them, him*, and *her* Read a short article Write a phone message (workbook)
Review	Review	Review

PREVIEW

FUNCTIONS/THEMES	LANGUAGE	FORMS
Introduce yourself	Hello. I'm Kenji Sato. Hi, Kenji. I'm Lauren Nash. My name is William Stone. Nice to meet you.	Present of *be:* (*am, is*) contractions
Identify people	Excuse me—are you Tom Cruise? Yes, I am. (No, I'm not.) What's your name, please?	Present of *be:* questions with *are;* short answers with *I*
Greet formally and informally	Hi, Maria. How are you? Not bad. Hello, Mrs. Baxter. How are you? I'm fine, Mr. Pierce.	More present of *be*
Verify a spelling	Could you spell your last name? N-I-E-L-S-E-N? Yes, that's right.	Alphabet Formula *Could you . . . ?*

Preview the conversations.

This is Carolyn Duval. She's moving from Vermont to New York. Carolyn is looking for an apartment today. She is at 3 Willow Street in Brooklyn, New York.

This is Mrs. Baxter. She's the landlady of 3 Willow Street.

1. Moving to a new city

Carolyn Duval finds a nice apartment.

A

Carolyn Duval Excuse me—
  are you Mrs. Baxter?
Woman No, I'm not.
Carolyn Sorry.

B

Carolyn Excuse me—are
  you Mrs. Baxter?
Mrs. Baxter Yes, I am.
Carolyn I'm Carolyn Duval.
Mrs. Baxter Nice to meet
  you, Ms. Duval.

C

Mrs. Baxter Let's see. . . .
  Carolyn . . . C-A-R-O-L-Y-N?
Carolyn Yes, that's right.
Mrs. Baxter Could you spell
  your last name, please?
Carolyn D-U-V-A-L.
Mrs. Baxter Sign here, please.

Maggie Sloane Hello, Mrs. Baxter.
Mrs. Baxter Oh, hello, Maggie. How are you?
Maggie Good. How are *you*?
Mrs. Baxter Fine, thanks.
Maggie Hi. Are you my new neighbor?
Carolyn Yes, I am. My name's Carolyn Duval.
Maggie I'm Maggie Sloane. I live upstairs in 3B.
Carolyn Nice to meet you, Maggie.
Maggie Nice to meet you, too, Carolyn.

Figure it out

1. Listen to the conversations. Say *true* or *false*.

1. Carolyn Duval meets Mrs. Baxter. *True*.
2. Carolyn's last name is Duval.
3. Carolyn lives upstairs from Maggie.
4. Carolyn is Maggie's neighbor.

2. Listen again. Match.

1. Are you Mrs. Baxter?   a. D-U-V-A-L.
2. Could you spell your last name?   b. *Carolyn Duval*
3. How are you?   c. No, I'm not.
4. C-A-R-O-L-Y-N?   d. C-A-R-O-L-Y-N.
5. Sign here, please.   e. Yes, that's right.
6. Could you spell your first name?   f. Fine.

3. Choose *a* or *b*.

1. Are you my new neighbor?
   a. Nice to meet you, too.
   (b.) Yes, I am.

2. D-U-V-A-L?
   a. Yes, I am.
   b. Yes, that's right.

3. Nice to meet you.
   a. Nice to meet you, too.
   b. My name's Sylvia Baxter.

4. My name's Carolyn Duval.
   a. Nice to meet you, Ms. Duval.
   b. Yes, that's right.

2. Nice to meet you.

1
- ▶ **Listen to the conversations below.**
- ▶ **Practice them with a partner. Use your own name.**
- ▶ **Introduce yourself to five classmates.**

Kenji Hello. I'm Kenji Sato.
Lauren Hi, Kenji. I'm Lauren Nash.

William Hello. My name's William Stone.
Vicky I'm Vicky Martinez.
William Nice to meet you, Vicky.
Vicky Nice to meet you, too.

Hi is more informal than **hello**.

INTRODUCE YOURSELF ● PRESENT OF *BE* (*AM*, *IS*): CONTRACTIONS

2 ▶ **Study the frames: Contractions**

I am	Maggie Sloane.
It is	nice to meet you.

→

I'm	Maggie Sloane.
It's	nice to meet you.

I'm and **it's** are contractions.
Nice to meet you = It's nice to meet you.

3 ▶ **Practice the conversation using contractions.**
▶ **Practice it again, using your own name.**

Maggie I am Maggie Sloane. *I'm Maggie Sloane.*
Carolyn My name is Carolyn Duval.
  I am your new neighbor.
Maggie It is nice to meet you, Carolyn.
Carolyn It is nice to meet you, too.

3. Are you Tom Cruise?

1 ► Your teacher will give you the names of three classmates. Find them and introduce yourself.

A Excuse me—are you _____ ?
B No, I'm not. I'm _____ .

A Excuse me—are you _____ ?
C Yes, I am.
A Hi. My name's _____ .
C Nice to meet you, _____ .
A Nice to meet you, too.

IDENTIFY SOMEONE ● PRESENT OF *BE* (*ARE*)

2 ► Study the frames: Present of *Be*

Yes-no questions	Short answers		Contraction	No contraction
Are you Tom Cruise?	Yes, **I am**.		No, **I'm not**.	Yes, **I am**.
	No, **I'm not**.			

3 ► Look at the photos. Then complete the conversations with the correct forms of the verb *be*. (To find out more about these famous people, see p. A87.)

1 Excuse me — *Are you* Tom Cruise?

Yes, *I am* .

2 Excuse me — _____ Whitney Houston?

No, _____ . _____ Janet Jackson.

3 Excuse me — _____ Yumi Matsutoya?

Yes, _____ . Nice to meet you.

4 Excuse me — _____ Julio Iglesias?

No, _____ . _____ Emmanuel.

4. How are you?

GREET SOMEONE INFORMALLY

1 ▶ **Listen to the conversation below.**
▶ **Greet several classmates.**

Maria Hello, Steve.
Steve Hi, Maria. How are you?
Maria Fine, thanks. How are *you*?
Steve Not bad.

How are you?	
Good.	O.K.
Fine.	Not bad.

GREET SOMEONE MORE FORMALLY

2 ▶ **Study the chart.**

First name	Carolyn	Sylvia	Charles
Title + last name	**Miss** [mɪs] Duval **Ms.** [mɪz] Duval	**Mrs.** Baxter **Ms.** Baxter	**Mr.** Baxter

Use **Miss** or **Ms.** with single women.
Use **Mrs.** or **Ms.** with married women.

3 ▶ **Listen to the conversations below. Complete them with first names or titles + last names.**
▶ **Greet your classmates using titles + last names.**

1

Hello, *Mr. Arno* .

Hi, *Jeff* . How are you?

Jeff Hunt

George Arno

2

Hi, _____ . How are you?

Not bad. How are you, _____ ?

George Arno

John Pierce

3

Hello, _____ . How are you today?

I'm fine, _____ . How are you?

John Pierce

Sylvia Baxter

4

Maggie Sloane

Hello, _____ . How are you?

Fine, thanks.

A 6 Unit 1

5. Could you spell your name?

Aa	Bb	Cc	Dd	Ee	Ff	Gg	Hh	Ii	Jj	Kk	Ll	Mm
Aa	*Bb*	*Cc*	*Dd*	*Ee*	*Ff*	*Gg*	*Hh*	*Ii*	*Jj*	*Kk*	*Ll*	*Mm*

Nn	Oo	Pp	Qq	Rr	Ss	Tt	Uu	Vv	Ww	Xx	Yy	Zz
Nn	*Oo*	*Pp*	*Qq*	*Rr*	*Ss*	*Tt*	*Uu*	*Vv*	*Ww*	*Xx*	*Yy*	*Zz*

1 ▸ **Listen to three conversations. Write each person's first and last name.**

1. _____
2. _____
3. _____

2 ▸ **Listen to the conversation below.**
▸ **Ask three classmates to spell their names.**

A What's your name, please?
B Chulsoo Kim.
A Could you spell your last name?
B K-I-M.
A And your first name?
B C-H-U-L-S-O-O.

VERIFY A SPELLING

3 ▸ **Listen to the two possible conversations below.**
▸ **Choose a first name and a last name from the box, and write the name on a piece of paper.**
▸ **Practice the conversation with a partner. Use your new name.**

A Your name, please?
|
B Robert Nielsen.

A N-I-E-L-S-E-N?   **A** N-I-E-L-S-O-N?
| |
B Yes, that's right. **B** No, N-I-E-L-S-*E*-N.

First name	Last name	Another spelling
Robert	Nielsen	Nielson
James	Lensky	Lenski
William	Allen	Allan
Nancy	Kramer	Cramer
Susan	Kelly	Kelley
Linda	Snyder	Snider

6. Welcome to Willow Street.

George Arno, owner of Arno's Coffee Shop, meets his new neighbor, Carolyn Duval.

1

George	Hi.
Carolyn	Hello.
George	Moving in?
Carolyn	Yes, I am.
George	Well then, we're neighbors. My name's George Arno and that's my coffee shop.
Carolyn	I'm Carolyn Duval. Nice to meet you.
George	Nice to meet you, too, Miss . . . uh . . . Laval?
Carolyn	No, *Du*val. But just call me Carolyn.
George	O.K., Carolyn. And you can call me George.
Loretta	GEORGE!
Jeff	Excuse me . . . uh . . . Mr. Arno, Mrs. Arno wants to . . .
Loretta	GEORGE!
George	Thanks, Jeff. COMING, LORETTA! Well, nice meeting you, Carolyn. Come in for coffee sometime.
Carolyn	Thank you. I will.

🔊 3. How to say it

Listen to this conversation.

Maggie Hi, my name's Maggie Sloane.

Carolyn Nice to meet you.

I'm Carolyn Duval.

2. Figure it out

True or *False?*

1. Carolyn is moving to Willow Street.
2. Carolyn is George Arno's new neighbor.
3. Carolyn's last name is Laval.
4. Mrs. Arno's first name is Loretta.
5. "Arno's" is a coffee shop on Willow Street.

🔊 4. Listen in

The man in the phone booth is making an appointment. Listen to the conversation. Spell the man's last name.

5. Your turn

Look at Maggie Sloane and her neighbor, John Pierce, above. Play the role of Maggie. Greet John.

7. Here I am in Kyoto!

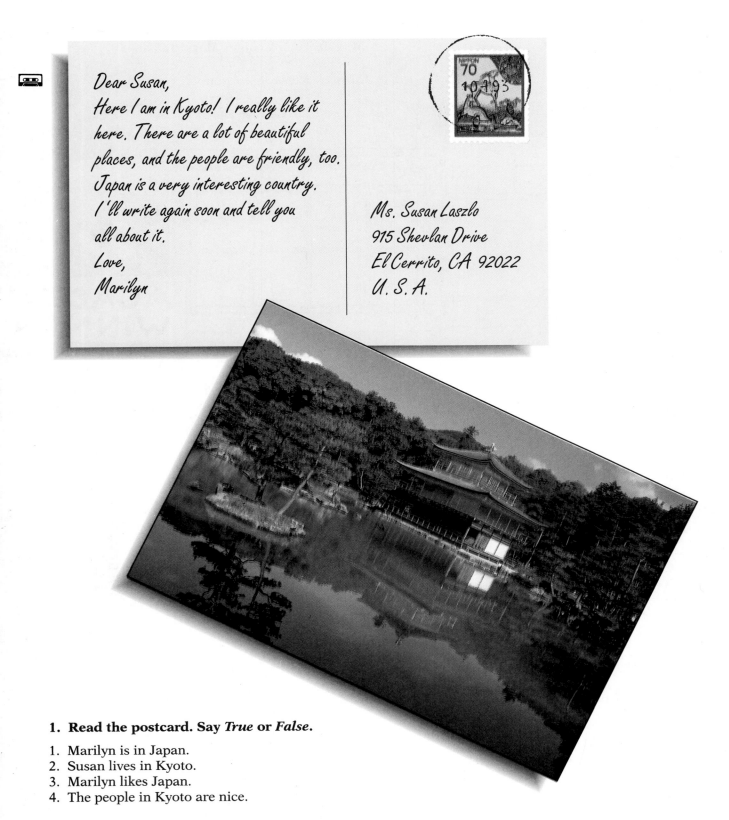

Dear Susan,

Here I am in Kyoto! I really like it here. There are a lot of beautiful places, and the people are friendly, too. Japan is a very interesting country. I'll write again soon and tell you all about it.

Love,
Marilyn

Ms. Susan Laszlo
915 Shevlan Drive
El Cerrito, CA 92022
U.S.A.

1. Read the postcard. Say *True* or *False*.

1. Marilyn is in Japan.
2. Susan lives in Kyoto.
3. Marilyn likes Japan.
4. The people in Kyoto are nice.

2. Find two reasons why Marilyn likes Kyoto.

PREVIEW

FUNCTIONS/THEMES	LANGUAGE	FORMS
Make an informal telephone call Identify someone on the phone	Is Susan there? Yes, she is. Just a minute, please. (No, she isn't.) Is this Bill? No, this is Carlos.	Present of *be: is* in yes-no questions and short answers
Ask for someone's phone number Call Directory Assistance Thank someone	What's your phone number? It's 555-2012. I'd like the number of Jane Schaefer. Thank you. You're welcome.	Numbers 0–10 Formula *I'd like* . . .
Ask for change	Excuse me—do you have change for a dollar? Yes, I do. Here you are. (No, I don't.)	Formulaic use of *do*
Apologize	I'm sorry. That's O.K.	

Preview the conversations.

a bill

a coin

a credit card

What's the problem with this telephone? Does this ever happen to you?

What do you need to use this telephone? A bill? A coin? A credit card? What about in your country?

8. Out of order

Bill is in town for the day, and he's trying to call his friend Susan.

A

Bill Excuse me, miss—do you have change for a dollar?
Woman Let's see. . . . No, I'm sorry, I don't.

B

Bill Sir? Do you have change for a dollar?
Man Uh . . . Let's see. . . . Ah, yes, I do. Here you are.
Bill Thank you.
Man You're welcome.

OUT OF ORDER

C

Operator Directory Assistance. May I help you?
Bill Yes. I'd like the number of Susan Chang, please— C-H-A-N-G.
Operator The number is 555-1037.
Bill 555-1037. Thank you.

D

Woman Hello?
Bill Hello, is Susan there?
Woman I'm sorry, you have the wrong number.
Bill Oh . . . is this 555-1037?
Woman No, it isn't.
Bill I'm sorry.
Woman That's O.K.

E

Susan's sister Hello?
Bill Hello, is Susan there?
Susan's sister No, I'm sorry, Susan isn't here right now. She's at work.

F

Susan's sister Hello?
Bill Hello, is Susan there?
Susan's sister Yes, she is. Just a minute, please.
Susan Hello?
Bill Hello, Susan? This is Bill.
Susan Bill?
Bill Bill Mitchell.
Susan Oh, hi, Bill! How . . . (*click!*)
Bill Hello?. . . Hello?

Uh . . . ma'am? Do you have change for a dollar?

Figure it out

1. Listen to the conversations. Say *true* or *false*.

1. Susan calls Bill.
2. Susan's number is 555-1037.
3. Bill is lucky today.

2. Listen again. Put the events in order.

___ Bill calls the wrong number.
___ Susan is there.
___ Susan is at work.
_1_ Bill wants change for a dollar.
___ Bill calls Directory Assistance.

3. Match.

1. Thank you.   a. No, it isn't.
2. Here you are.   b. You're welcome.
3. I'm sorry.   c. That's O.K.
4. Is this 555-6696?   d. No, I don't.
5. Do you have change   e. Thank you.
   for a dollar?

4. Look at the picture below. Choose *a* or *b*.

1. Change for a dollar is _____ .
   a. 8 dimes and 2 nickels
   b. 4 quarters

2. Change for a quarter is _____ .
   a. 2 dimes and 1 nickel
   b. 4 nickels

a quarter
25 cents

a dime
10 cents

a nickel
5 cents

a penny
1 cent

9. Phone calls

 1 ▶ Complete the phone conversations below with *a*, *b*, or *c*.
▶ Listen to the conversations to check your answers.
▶ Practice them with a partner.

a. No, she isn't here right now. She's at work.
b. This is Susan.
c. Yes, she is. Just a minute, please.

MAKE A CALL • PRESENT OF *BE* (*IS*)

2 ▶ Study the frames.
▶ Practice the conversations in exercise 1 again. This time ask for Bill.

Yes-no questions			Short answers				Negative statements			Affirmative statements		
Is	Bill	there?	Yes,	he	**is.**		He	**isn't**	here.	He	**'s**	at work.
	Susan		No,	she	**isn't.**		She			She		

's = is
isn't = is not

You may say:
he isn't or **he's not**.
she isn't or **she's not**.

CALL YOUR CLASSMATES

3 ▶ Act out this conversation in groups of three using your own names.

A (*Dials number*) Rrring, rrring
B Hello?
A Hello, is _____ there?
B Yes, he (she) is. Just a minute, please.
C Hello?
A Hello, _____ ? This is _____ .
C Oh, hi, _____ . How are you?
A Fine, thanks. How are you?
C Not bad.

4 ▶ **Study the frames.**

	Are you Bill?	Yes, I am.
		No, I'm Carlos.
	Is this Bill?	Yes, it is.
		No, this is Carlos.
		No, it's Carlos.

It usually refers to a thing and takes the same form of the verb as *he* and *she*:

Is your number 555-1037?	Yes, **it is**.
Is your number 555-1032?	No, **it isn't**. **It's** 555-1037.

5 ▶ **Complete the conversations.**

1. **George** Hello?
   Phil Hello, is George there?
   George ___*This is*___ George.
   Phil Hi, George. _____ Phil Wang.
   George Phil Wang?
   Phil _____ George Dobbs?
   George No. _____ George Arno.

2. **Carolyn** ___*Are you*___ Jeff Hunt?
   Jeff Yes, _____ .
   Carolyn Nice to meet you, Jeff. _____
   Carolyn Duval. Is George Arno here?
   Jeff No, _____ .

 6 ▶ **Put the lines of the conversations below in order.**
▶ **Listen to the conversations to check your work.**
▶ **Act out the conversations using your own names.**

1. ___ Bill?
   ___ That's O.K.
   _1_ Hello?
   _2_ Hello, Susan? This is Bill.
   ___ I'm sorry.
   ___ Is this Susan Chang?
   ___ No. You have the wrong number.

2. ___ Hello, is this Susan?
   ___ Hi, Jane. This is Bill.
   Is Susan there?
   ___ Hello?
   ___ No, it isn't. This is Jane.
   ___ No, she isn't here right now. She's at work.

3. ___ Hi, Susan. This is Bill.
   ___ Hello?
   ___ Yes, it is.
   ___ Bill! How are you?
   ___ Hello, is this Susan?
   ___ Great.

10. Numbers

0	1	2	3	4	5	6	7	8	9	10
zero	one	two	three	four	five	six	seven	eight	nine	ten

1 ▶ **Listen to these phone numbers. Then say them.**

1. 555-4481
2. 555-7023
3. 555-9444
4. 555-4917
5. 555-1038
6. 555-3394
7. 555-0384
8. 555-4901

> Zero is pronounced "oh" when saying a phone number.

2 ▶ **Practice saying the numbers on the passports and credit card.**

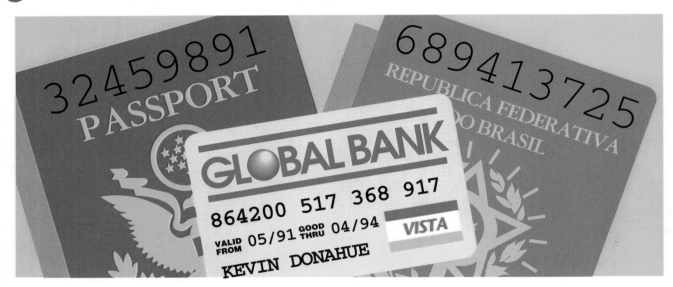

ASK FOR SOMEONE'S PHONE NUMBER

3 ▶ **Marco is taking orders for pizzas. Listen to the conversations and write down the phone numbers.**

1. _____
2. _____
3. _____
4. _____

4 ▶ **Listen to the conversation below.**
▶ **Ask three classmates for their phone numbers. Write down the numbers and confirm them.**

A What's your phone number?
B It's 555-2012.
A 555-2102?
B No. It's 555-2012.
A 555-2012.
B That's right.

11. Phone frustrations

CALL DIRECTORY ASSISTANCE

 1 ▶ **Listen to the conversation below.**

A (*Dials number*) *Rrring, rrring*
B Directory Assistance.
A I'd like the number of Jane Schaefer.
A Could you spell the last name, please?
B S-C-H-A-E-F-E-R.
A The number is 555-5275.
B Thank you.
A You're welcome.

▶ **Play these roles:**

Student A You need to call someone in the list, but you don't have the phone number. Call Directory Assistance.

Student B Play the role of the operator. Use the information in the list.

Sanchez Pedro 315 Washington	555-9821
Sato Aki 915 River Avenue	555-3004
Schaefer Jane 201 W 23 St	555-5275
Scott John R 910 Union St	555-3003
Scotto Julia 1785 Park Road	555-0403
Shafer L A 111 W 48 St	555-8707
Shaw Anne 915 River Avenue	555-3924
Shaw James 425 Adams St	555-0862
Shin Young 202 E 28 St	555-1343
Silva Paul 522 California	555-4508
Silver Frank 647 Second Ave	555-3473
Simmons J B 2665 Lake Road	555-1159
Small Carolyn 407 Lincoln St	555-2683
Smith Carl 809 River Avenue	555-6182
Smith David 505 E 32 St	555-7396
Smith Nancy 10 Wilson St	555-6936
Smith Robert 924 Third Avenue	555-3254
Stavros Tony 812 Union St	555-4829
Sullivan Jean 21 E 19 St	555-9821

ASK FOR CHANGE

 2 ▶ **You need change to make a phone call. Listen to the two conversations below.**
▶ **Find a classmate who can give you change.**

A Excuse me—do you have change for a dollar?
B Let's see. . . . No, I'm sorry, I don't.

A Excuse me—do you have change for a dollar?
C Yes, I do. Here you are.
A Thanks.
C You're welcome.

Thank you is more formal than **thanks**.

APOLOGIZE FOR A WRONG NUMBER

3 ▶ **Work in small groups. Sit with your back to the group and call someone in it. If you get a wrong number, call again.**

A (*Dials number*) *Rrring, rrring*
B Hello?
A Hello, is _____ there?
B No, you have the wrong number.
A Is this __(number)__ ?
B No, it isn't.
A I'm sorry.
B That's O.K.
A (*Dials again*) *Rrring, rrring*

12. Arno's Coffee Shop

John Pierce stops in to have a cup of coffee at Arno's.

1

George Hi, John! Come on in and sit down.

John Hi, George. How are you?

George Good. How about you?

John I'm fine, thanks.

George John, do you know Nick Pappas? He has a grocery store down the street.

John No, I don't. Nice to meet you, Nick. I'm John Pierce.

Nick Hi, John.

George John is a neighbor. He lives next door. Coffee, John?

John Yes, please.

George More coffee, Nick?

Nick No, thanks, George. I have to go. Good-bye, John. Nice meeting you.

John Bye, Nick.

George See you, Nick. (*To John*) So, John, how's your new neighbor?

John My new neighbor?

George Yes — Carolyn Duval. She just moved into your building.

John Oh, yeah — into the apartment upstairs. . . . I don't know her.

George Oh, she's very nice. . . .

2. Figure it out

True or *False?*

1. John meets Nick Pappas.
2. Nick Pappas works on Willow Street.
3. John knows Carolyn Duval.
4. Carolyn Duval lives upstairs from John.

 **3. Listen in**

The man below is trying to call a friend, but the number has been changed. Listen and write down the friend's new telephone number.

 5. How to say it

Listen to this conversation.

A Hello?

B Hello, is Susan there?

A Susan?

B Is this 555-1032?

A No, it isn't.

6. Your turn

The man below needs some change. Act out his conversation with Loretta Arno.

4. Your turn

The woman above is calling a friend and gets the wrong number. Act out a possible conversation.

Woman *(Dials number.)* Rrring, rrring
Man Hello?
Woman _____?
Man I'm sorry, you have the wrong number.
Woman _____?
Man No, it's 555-9904.
Woman _____.
Man That's O.K.

13. 📼

Is the telephone your friend or your enemy?

Lisa Daoud
High School Student

The telephone is my _friend_! I love to talk to my friends on the telephone.

Louis Sanchez
Architect

It's my _enemy_! People call me with bad news and more work!

Ashok Gupta
Retired Doctor

Oh, it's my FRIEND. A telephone is very important in an emergency.

Arthur Shawcross
Construction Worker

The telephone is definitely my ENEMY! It's expensive and my telephone is often out of order.

Evelyn Pollack
Housewife

The telephone is my good FRIEND! I have six children and I need a telephone. Believe me!

Rika Ito
Potter

Oh, it's not my FRIEND It's my enemy. People always call when I'm in the shower or asleep.

1. **Read the article. Then fill in each blank with "friend" or "enemy."**

2. **What's your opinion? Is the telephone your friend or your enemy?**

PREVIEW

FUNCTIONS/THEMES	LANGUAGE	FORMS
Ask about the location of cities Ask where people are from	Where's Tokyo? In Japan. Where are you from? I'm from Brazil. The Lopezes are from Mexico.	Present of *be*: information questions; statements; yes-no questions and short answers Plural of names
Introduce people	Tony, this is my friend, Linda. Linda, this is Tony.	
Offer something to drink	Do you want some coffee? Yes, please. (No, thank you.)	Formulaic use of *do*
Say good-bye after meeting someone	Good-bye. Nice meeting you.	
Ask for someone's address	What's Jim's address? It's 60 Bank Street. Sixty or sixteen? Sixty—six-oh	Numbers 11–100 Possessive of names

Preview the conversations.

Carlos is flying to New York. Where is he from?

Carlos is at a friend's house in New York. His friend is offering him something to drink. What is it? What do you normally offer your friends?

14. Where are you from?

Carlos Gomez is going to New York to visit his friends Betty and Jim Fox.

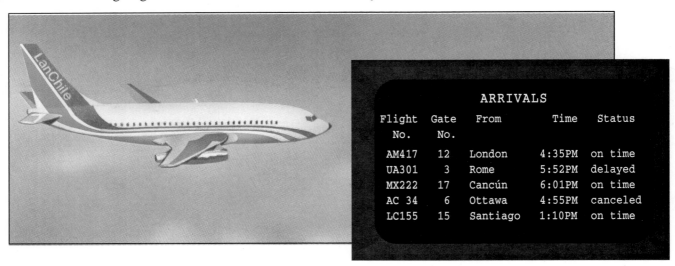

Flight No.	Gate No.	From	Time	Status
AM417	12	London	4:35PM	on time
UA301	3	Rome	5:52PM	delayed
MX222	17	Cancún	6:01PM	on time
AC 34	6	Ottawa	4:55PM	canceled
LC155	15	Santiago	1:10PM	on time

ARRIVALS

A

Carlos 60 Bank Street, please.
Cab driver Sixty or sixteen?
Carlos Sixty—six-oh.
Cab driver Bank Street . . . let's see. . . .
Is that near Waverly Place?
Carlos I don't know. This is my first trip to
New York.
Cab driver Oh? Where are you from?
Carlos Chile.
Cab driver Where in Chile?
Carlos Santiago.

B

Betty Carlos! You're here!
Carlos Betty! Jim! How are you?
Jim We're fine. How about you?
Carlos Great! It's good to be here finally.

Jim Carlos, this is my sister, Karen. Karen, this is Carlos—an old friend from school.
Carlos Hi, Karen.
Karen Nice to meet you, Carlos.

Jim Do you want some coffee, Carlos?
Carlos Yes, please.
Jim Cream and sugar?
Carlos No, thanks.

Karen Good-bye, everyone.
Betty, Jim, Carlos Bye.
Karen Nice meeting you, Carlos.
Carlos Nice meeting you, too.

Figure it out

1. Listen to the conversations. What city is Carlos from?

2. Listen again. Say *true* or *false*.

1. Jim and Betty live in Santiago.
2. Jim and Betty live on Bank Street.
3. Betty is Jim's wife.
4. Carlos is Karen's friend from school.
5. Karen is Jim's sister.

3. Choose *a* or *b*.

1. We're fine. How about you?
   a. Great.
   b. You're here!

2. Good-bye.
   a. Nice meeting you.
   b. Nice to meet you, too.

3. Karen, this is Carlos. Carlos, Karen.
   a. Nice to meet you.
   b. Nice meeting you.

4. Cream and sugar?
   a. Do you want some coffee?
   b. Yes, please.

15. The Silvas are from Brazil.

CITIES AND COUNTRIES

See p. A86 for a complete list of countries.

1 ► **Ask and answer questions about the location of the cities below.**

A Where's Tokyo?
B In Japan.

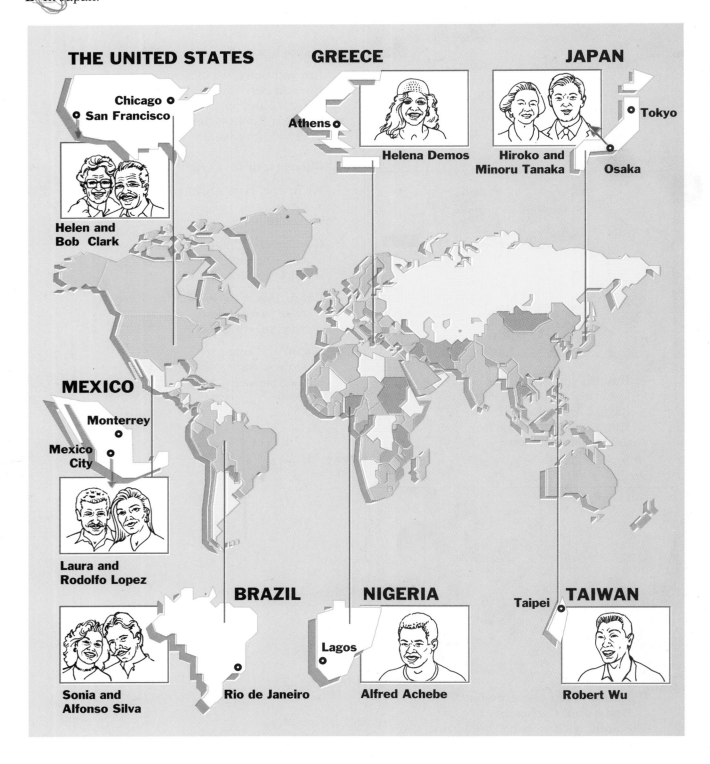

THE UNITED STATES

Chicago ○
○ San Francisco

Helen and
Bob Clark

GREECE

Athens ○

Helena Demos

JAPAN

○ Tokyo

Hiroko and
Minoru Tanaka

Osaka ○

MEXICO

Monterrey
○

Mexico
City ○

Laura and
Rodolfo Lopez

BRAZIL

○ Rio de Janeiro

NIGERIA

Lagos ○

Alfred Achebe

Taipei ○ **TAIWAN**

Robert Wu

Sonia and
Alfonso Silva

SAY WHAT COUNTRY PEOPLE ARE FROM

 2 ▶ Listen to the pronunciation of the plural names in the box.

▶ Say what countries the people on the map on p. A24 are from. For married couples, use the plural form of their names.

The Silvas are from Brazil.

Helen and Bob Clark	→ the Clark**s**	[s]
Sonia and Alfonso Silva	→ the Silva**s**	[z]
Laura and Rodolfo Lopez	→ the Lopez**es**	[ɪz]

ch, **sh**, **s**, **z**, **x**: Add **-es**.

ASK WHAT CITY AND COUNTRY PEOPLE ARE FROM ● PRESENT OF *BE*

 3 ▶ Study the frames: Present of *Be*

Information questions				Statements				Yes-no questions				Short answers		
	are	you		I	**'m**			**Are**	you			Yes,	I	**am.**
		they							they			No,		**'m not.**
Where			from?	We They	**'re**	from Japan.				from Tokyo?		Yes,	we	**are.**
	is	he						**Is**	he			No,	they	**aren't.**
		she		He She	**'s**				she			Yes,	he	**is.**
												No,	she	**isn't.**

You may say:

we aren't or **we're not.**
they aren't or **they're not.**

 4 ▶ The people on the map are on vacation together. Listen to the conversation below.

Robert Wu Sonia, where are you and Alfonso from?
Sonia Silva We're from Brazil.
Robert Wu Oh, are you from Rio?
Sonia Silva Yes, we are.
Robert Wu And the Lopezes—are they from Brazil, too?
Sonia Silva No, they aren't. They're from Mexico.

▶ **Play these roles:**

Student A Ask where the people below are from. Don't look at the map.
Student B Use the information on the map to answer Student A's questions.

Robert Wu	Sonia and Alfonso Silva	Laura and Rodolfo Lopez
Hiroko and Minoru Tanaka	Helena Demos	Helen and Bob Clark

FIND OUT WHERE YOUR CLASSMATES ARE FROM

 5 ▶ Listen to the conversations below. Fill in the blanks with the correct city or country.
▶ Practice the conversations in small groups. Use personal information.

1. **A** Where are you from?
   B I'm from _____ . How about you?
   A I'm from _____ .

2. **A** Where are you from?
   B I'm from _____ .
   A Oh, I'm from _____ , too.

16. Socializing

GREETINGS AND INTRODUCTIONS

 1
► The people in the picture above are at a party. Listen to the conversations.
► Imagine you're at a party with students from your school. Greet a friend.
► Introduce another student to your friend.
► Introduce yourself to someone you don't know.

OFFER SOMETHING TO DRINK

2
► Listen to the two possible conversations below.
► Offer another student something to drink.

A Do you want some coffee?

B Yes, please.   **B** No, thanks.
                  A How about some tea?
                  B O.K. Thanks.

coffee   tea   water   milk   soda

SAY GOOD-BYE AFTER MEETING SOMEONE

3
► Say good-bye to the classmates you met today.

Linda Good-bye, Tony. Nice meeting you.
Tony Bye, Linda. Nice meeting you, too.

> When you first meet someone, say "Nice to meet you."
> When you say good-bye, say "Nice meeting you."

17. Addresses

NUMBERS: 11–100

11	12	13	14	15	16	17	18	19	20
eleven	twelve	thirteen	fourteen	fifteen	sixteen	seventeen	eighteen	nineteen	twenty

21	30	40	50	60	70	80	90	100
twenty-one	thirty	forty	fifty	sixty	seventy	eighty	ninety	one hundred

 1 ▶ **Which number do you hear? Choose *a* or *b*.**

1. a. 13 b. 30   3. a. 19 b. 90   5. a. 15 b. 50   7. a. 17 b. 70
2. a. 16 b. 60   4. b. 14 b. 40   6. a. 18 b. 80   8. a. 12 b. 20

ASK FOR SOMEONE'S ADDRESS

2 ▶ **Listen to the addresses on the mailing labels.**
   ▶ **Practice conversations like the one below, using the addresses on the labels.**

A What's Jim's address?
B It's 60 Bank Street.
A Sixty or sixteen?
B Sixty—six-oh.

Possessives of names are pronounced like plurals of names:

Pat**'s** address   [s]
John**'s** address   [z]
Liz**'s** address   [ɪz]

114 is said "one-fourteen."

Mr. Jim Fox
60 Bank Street
New York, NY 10014
U.S.A.

Ms. Roberta Tudhope
17 Hyde Park Street
Toronto, Ont. M65 1M5
CANADA

Mr. Gary Cooke
30 Bryan Road
London W7H 7F8
ENGLAND

Ms. Ann O'Reilly
114 Lakeland Street
Kilmacud, Blackrock
County Dublin Ireland

Mr. Tim Rogers   2011
619 King Avenue
New South Wales
AUSTRALIA

ADD SOMEONE TO YOUR ADDRESS BOOK

3 ▶ **Listen to the conversation below.**

A What's your address, Carol?
B 1430 Langdon Street. L-A-N-G-D-O-N.
A And what's your phone number?
B 555-8214.
A And your last name is Merrill?
B Right. M-E-R-R-I-L-L.
A Thanks.

▶ Using the questions below, find out the full names, addresses, and phone numbers of three students. Write them in your address book.
▶ Verify that your information is correct.

Carol Merrill
1430 Langdon Street
Los Angeles, CA 90063 U.S.A.
213-555-8214

Nestor Morales
Cerro del Borrego 135
Copilco, D.F. 31245 MEXICO
52-5-555-6528

Helen Murata
872 Lake Road
Willowdale, Ont. M2C 2H8 CANADA
615-555-7778

What's your address?
What's your phone number?
What's your last name?
Could you spell that?
What's the number again?
Is this right?

18. Laundromat

Loretta Arno runs into Stella Pappas, Nick's wife, in the laundromat.

1

Stella Hi, Loretta!

Loretta Stella, hi! How are you?

Stella Oh, not bad—a little tired. Oh, Loretta, I'd like you to meet my brother-in-law.

Alex Nice to meet you. My name's Alex.

Loretta I'm sorry, did you say Alec or Alex?

Alex Alex—with an "x."

Loretta Well, it's nice to meet you, Alex. Your brother, Nick, and my husband, George, are very good friends.

Stella Loretta and George own Arno's Coffee Shop down the street.

Alex Oh . . .

Loretta Where are you from, Alex?

Alex I'm from Athens, Te . . .

Loretta Athens! How nice! I'd like to go to Greece someday. I bet it's beautiful there.

Alex Oh, no—not Athens, Greece. I'm from Athens, Texas.

2. Figure it out

True or *False*? **Correct the false statements.**

1. Stella and Loretta are friends.
2. Nick is Stella's husband.
3. Alex is Stella's brother.
4. Alex is from Athens, Greece.

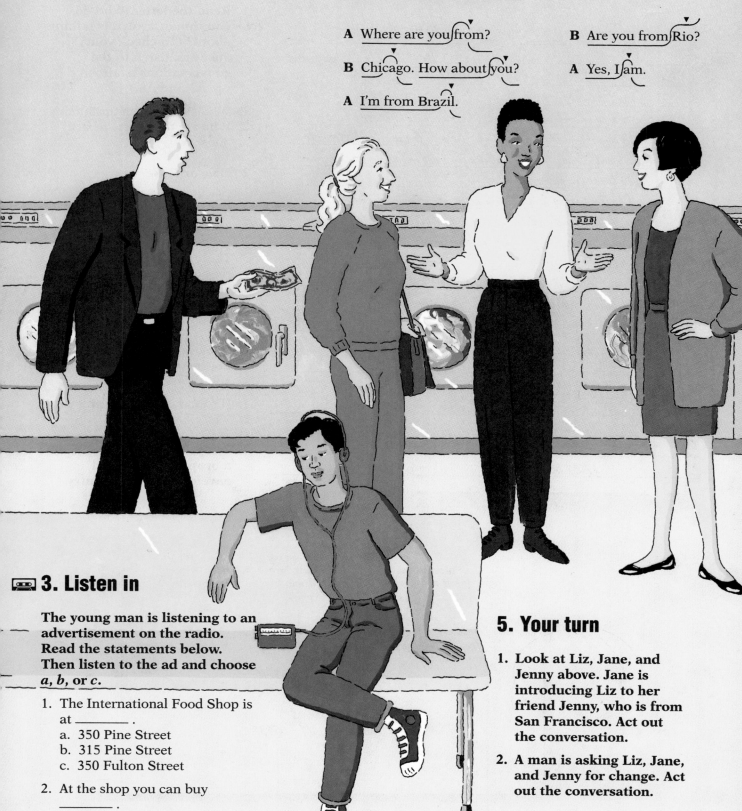

▥ 4. How to say it

Listen to this conversation.

A Where are you from?

B Chicago. How about you?

A I'm from Brazil.

B Are you from Rio?

A Yes, I am.

▥ 3. Listen in

The young man is listening to an advertisement on the radio. Read the statements below. Then listen to the ad and choose *a*, *b*, or *c*.

1. The International Food Shop is at _____ .
   a. 350 Pine Street
   b. 315 Pine Street
   c. 350 Fulton Street

2. At the shop you can buy _____ .
   a. bread and cheese
   b. coffee and tea
   c. cream and sugar

5. Your turn

1. Look at Liz, Jane, and Jenny above. Jane is introducing Liz to her friend Jenny, who is from San Francisco. Act out the conversation.

2. A man is asking Liz, Jane, and Jenny for change. Act out the conversation.

19. My new address and phone number are . . .

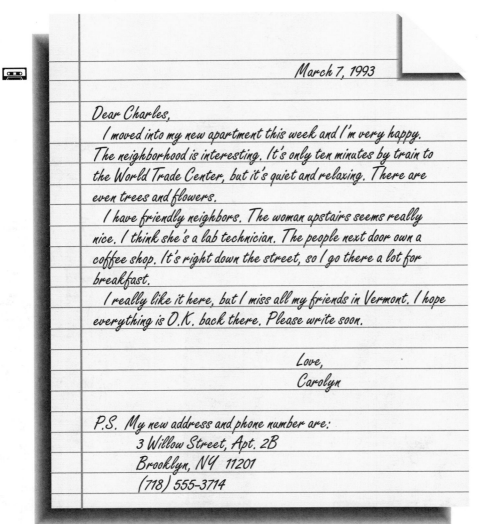

March 7, 1993

Dear Charles,

I moved into my new apartment this week and I'm very happy. The neighborhood is interesting. It's only ten minutes by train to the World Trade Center, but it's quiet and relaxing. There are even trees and flowers.

I have friendly neighbors. The woman upstairs seems really nice. I think she's a lab technician. The people next door own a coffee shop. It's right down the street, so I go there a lot for breakfast.

I really like it here, but I miss all my friends in Vermont. I hope everything is O.K. back there. Please write soon.

Love,
Carolyn

P.S. My new address and phone number are:
3 Willow Street, Apt. 2B
Brooklyn, NY 11201
(718) 555-3714

1. Read the letter. Who do you think Carolyn is talking about? (To check your answers, listen to the conversations again on pp. A3 and A8.)

1. Who's the woman upstairs?
2. Who are the people next door?

2. *True* or *False*?

1. Carolyn's neighborhood is quiet and relaxing.
2. The World Trade Center is in her neighborhood.
3. There's a coffee shop down the street from Carolyn's apartment.
4. Charles is a friend from Vermont.

3. Look at the envelope. What do these abbreviations stand for?

1. NY *New York*   3. Apt.
2. VT   4. S.

4. Compare the envelope to a properly addressed envelope in your country.

Include the
apartment number.

Is it Street, Avenue, Drive,
Road, Place, or Boulevard?

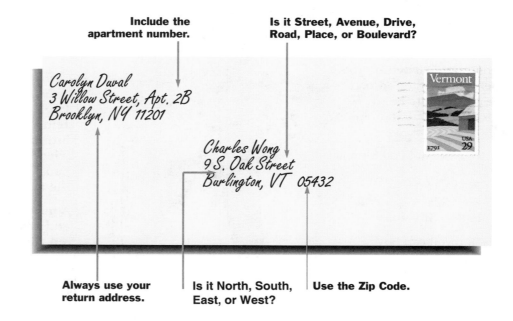

Carolyn Duval
3 Willow Street, Apt. 2B
Brooklyn, NY 11201

Charles Wong
9 S. Oak Street
Burlington, VT 05432

Always use your
return address.

Is it North, South,
East, or West?

Use the Zip Code.

FUNCTIONS/THEMES	LANGUAGE	FORMS
Give locations in a neighborhood	Excuse me—is the post office near here? Where's the post office, please? On Second Avenue./Between Main and High Streets./Across from the park./ Next to the restaurant./On the corner of Second and High.	Prepositions of place
Give locations in an apartment building	Where's the Brunis' apartment? On the first floor.	Ordinal numbers 1st–10th Possessive of names
Give directions in a neighborhood	Walk to the corner. Go straight ahead for two blocks. Turn right/left.	Imperative Adverbs of location

Preview the conversations.

Bill Hinko is looking for something. What is it?

What's Bill's problem? Does this ever happen to you?

20. Where's the post office?

Bill Hinko has just moved to Greenville and is trying to find the post office.

A

Bill Excuse me—where's the post office, please?

Woman Hmm . . . I think it's that way. Or is it that way? I'm not sure.

B

Bill Excuse me—where's the post office?

Man That way.

Woman No, dear, it's that way.

Man Honey, you're wrong. The post office is on Second Avenue, next to Fred's Restaurant.

Woman No, it's not, dear. It's on the corner of State and Fifth.

Man No, dear . . .

C

Bill Excuse me—is the post office near here?

Man I'm sorry, I don't know.

Bill Thanks anyway.

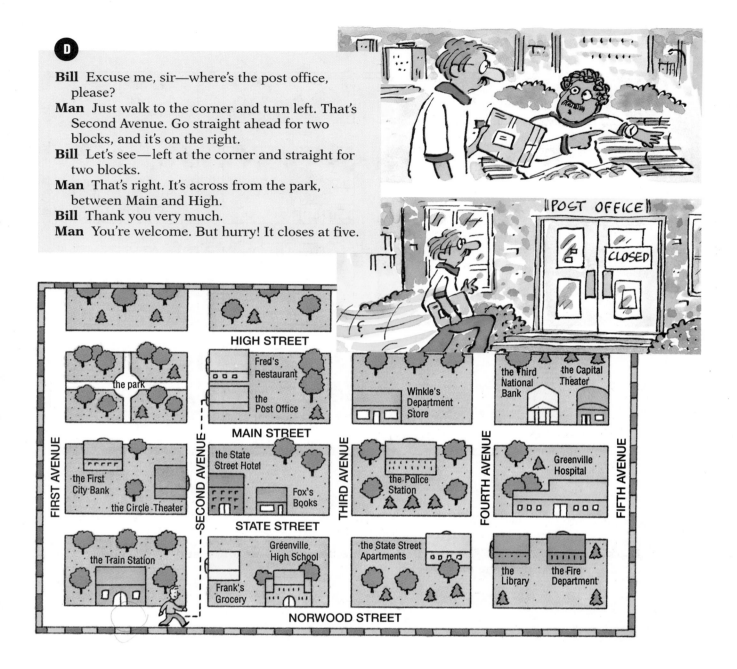

D

Bill Excuse me, sir—where's the post office, please?

Man Just walk to the corner and turn left. That's Second Avenue. Go straight ahead for two blocks, and it's on the right.

Bill Let's see—left at the corner and straight for two blocks.

Man That's right. It's across from the park, between Main and High.

Bill Thank you very much.

Man You're welcome. But hurry! It closes at five.

Figure it out

1. Read the sentences below. Then listen to the conversations and complete the sentences.

1. The post office is on _____ Avenue.
2. It's between _____ Street and _____ Street.
3. It closes at _____ o'clock.

2. Follow your teacher's commands.

1. Stand up.
2. Turn right.
3. Walk straight ahead.
4. Go to the door.
5. Go to the board.
6. Turn left.
7. Go to your seat.
8. Sit down.

3. Using the map of Greenville above, complete these sentences.

1. Fred's Restaurant is next to _the post office_ .
2. The post office is across from _____ .
3. The fire department is across from _____ .
4. _____ is on the corner of State and Fifth.
5. Fox's Books is next to _____ .
6. Frank's Grocery is on _____ Avenue, between _____ Street and _____ Street .

21. Locations and directions

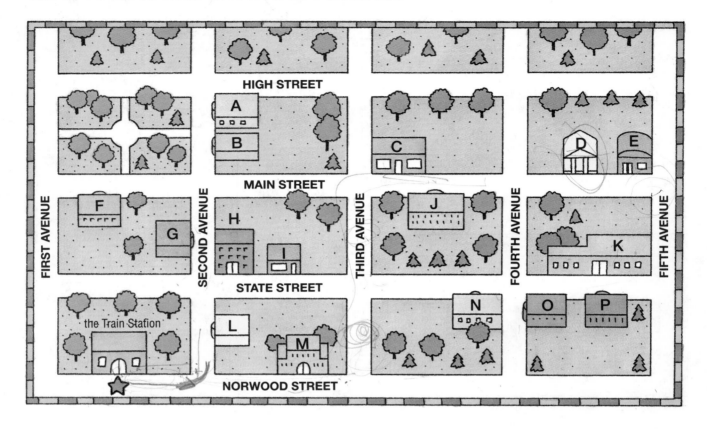

HIGH STREET

MAIN STREET

STATE STREET

NORWOOD STREET

FIRST AVENUE

SECOND AVENUE

THIRD AVENUE

FOURTH AVENUE

FIFTH AVENUE

the Train Station

TALK ABOUT LOCATION ● PREPOSITIONS OF PLACE

1 ► Look at the map above. Then study the frame. Find the post office and
Fred's Restaurant on the map.

The post office is **on** Second Avenue.
It's on Second **between** Main and High.
It's **across from** the park.
It's **next to** Fred's Restaurant.
Fred's Restaurant is **on the corner of** Second and High.

LOCATIONS

2 ► Listen to the conversation below.

A Where's the post office, please?
B It's on Second Avenue, between Main and High.
A (*Repeats*) Second Avenue between Main and High.
B That's right.
A Thank you very much.

► **Play these roles:**

Student A Ask where the places in the box are located.
Then find them on the map above.

Student B Using the map on p. A33, answer Student A's questions.

Some places

the post office
the First City Bank
Greenville High School
the Circle Theater
the fire department
the Third National Bank
Fox's Books
Winkle's Department Store
Greenville Hospital
the library

3 ▶ Study the frame: The Imperative   🔊 **4** ▶ Four people are at the train station and are asking directions to the places below. Look at the map on p. A34 as you listen to the conversations. Then find each place on the map.

> **Walk** to the corner of Second and State.
> **Go** straight ahead for two blocks.
> **Turn** right (left).

Directions.

▶ Look at the map on p. A33 to check your answers.

1. _H_ the State Street Hotel   3. ____ the police station
2. ____ Frank's Grocery   4. ____ the Capital Theater

🔊 **5** ▶ A tourist is asking directions to Greenville Hospital. As you listen to the conversation below, fill in the blanks.
▶ Where's the tourist? Check your answer on p. A33.

A Excuse me—is Greenville Hospital near here?
B Yes, it is. Walk to the _____ and turn _____ on _____.
Go straight ahead for _____ blocks. The hospital is on the _____ .
A Thank you very much.
B You're welcome.

6 ▶ Ask a classmate directions to a place on the map. Start at the following locations:

1. the post office   2. Winkle's Department Store   3. the library   4. the park

7 ▶ Study the numbers. Then study the frames below: Possessives of Names

1st	2nd	3rd	4th	5th	6th	7th	8th	9th	10th
first	second	third	fourth	fifth	sixth	seventh	eighth	ninth	tenth

Singular	Philip Tate's	[s]	apartment	Ann Bruni's	[z]	apartment	Doris Fox's	[ɪz]	apartment
Plural	the Tates'			the Brunis'			the Foxes'		

8 ▶ Find the State Street Apartments on the corner of State and Fourth. Then ask and answer questions like this:

A Where's the Brunis' apartment?
B It's on the fourth floor. Apartment 4F.

Ann and Jack Bruni	4F
Rosa Cela	9D
the Chungs	10C
Carmen Contreras	3B
Peter Dodge	2C
Bill and Doris Fox	7A
Nancy Frank	6B
John Hong	8E
the McCoys	1D
Philip and Jane Tate	1A

22. What's in the neighborhood?

1 ► How many of these places are in the neighborhood near your school? Make a chart, like the one on the right, and write down the names of the places. Do not fill in the locations.

PLACE	LOCATION
1. the Taj Mahal Restaurant	
2. the Good Food Grocery	
3. Mel's Hardware	
4. Sunnyview Park	
5. Paradise Disco	

a hotel

a hardware store

a theater

a clothing store

a park

a record store

a grocery store

a good restaurant

► Exchange charts with another student, and find a classmate who can give you directions to each place. Write down the locations.
► Share the information with other students or with the whole class.

A Excuse me—is _____ near here?
B I'm sorry, I don't know.
A Thanks anyway. . . .

A Excuse me—is _____ near here?
C Yes, it is. Just _____ . _____ is on the _____ .
A Let's see. . . . It's on _____ Street.
C That's right.
A Thanks a lot.

a discotheque

23. Map mystery

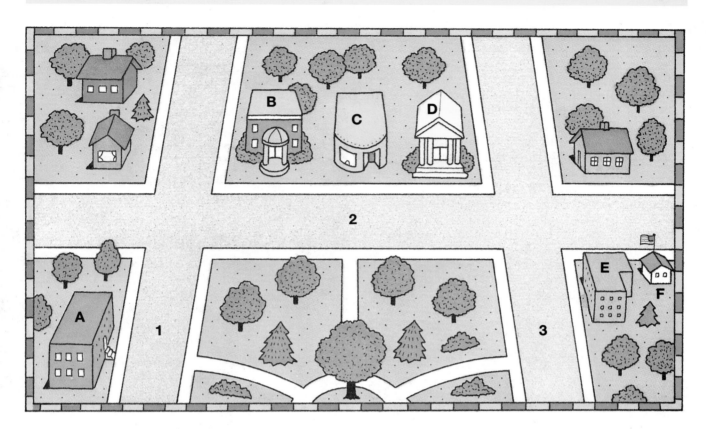

1 ▶ **Find the buildings and streets on the map of Glenwood above. The buildings are labeled A, B, C, D, E, and F, and the streets are numbered 1, 2, and 3. Use the clues below.**

Clues:

1. The Oak Street Theater is not on a corner.
   Hint: *The Oak Street Theater is A, C, or F.*
2. The Oak Street Theater is across from the park.
3. The Oak Street Theater is between the Glenwood Savings Bank and the library.
4. The police station is across from the park.
5. The post office is next to the police station.
6. You're at the post office. Turn left, walk to the corner, and turn left. You're on Walnut.
7. The library is not on the corner of Oak and Walnut.
8. You're at the Oak Street Theater. Turn right and walk to the corner. Turn left on Elm. The hospital is on your right.

Buildings	Streets
the Oak Street Theater	Oak Street
the Glenwood Savings Bank	Walnut Street
the library	Elm Street
the police station	
the post office	
the hospital	

Answers to Exercise 1

A. the hospital	1. Elm Street
B. the library	2. Oak Street
C. the Oak Street Theater	3. Walnut Street
D. the Glenwood Savings Bank	
E. the police station	
F. the post office	

24. Traffic jam

John Pierce offers Maggie Sloane a ride to the bank, but Maggie finds out that sometimes it's faster to walk.

1

John	Maggie!
Maggie	Oh, John . . . hi, how are you? Listen, I'm in a terrible hurry. The bank closes in fifteen minutes.
John	Is your bank near here?
Maggie	Yes, it's only three blocks away—on Fulton Street.
John	Well, get in. I'll take you.
Maggie	Are you sure? It's not out of your way?
John	No, not at all.
Maggie	This is so nice of you, John. Thank you.
John	Don't mention it.
Maggie	Say, this is a nice car!
John	Yeah, it's my brother's. He's away for a month.

2

John	Now let's see. . . . Fulton Street is that way . . .
Maggie	Yes, just turn right at the next corner.
John	That's a one-way street.
Maggie	Oh, you're right. Well, turn right at this corner.
John	I'm in the wrong lane. Well, let's see. . . . Maybe I can . . .
Cab driver	What are you doing? Are you crazy or something?
John	Oh, this traffic is terrible!
Maggie	You know what? I think I'll walk. But thanks anyway.

3. Figure it out

1. *True* or *False*?

1. Maggie is not in a hurry.
2. Maggie's bank is on Fulton Street.
3. The car is John's.
4. John is in the wrong lane to turn right.
5. Maggie walks to the bank.

4. How to say it

Listen to the pronounciation of the words below. Then listen to the conversation.

Arno's	Mitch's	Pat's
[z]	[ɪz]	[s]

A I'd like a taxi at Arno's Coffee Shop.
B A taxi?
A Is this 555-3822?
B Yes, it is.
A And it's not Mitch's Taxi?
B No, it's not. It's Pat's Restaurant.

5. Your turn

The man in the car wants to go to the post office on Montague Street. Find the post office in the picture. Then act out his conversation with the other man.

Excuse me—where's the post office, please? . . .

6. Listen in

The man on the motorcycle is asking for directions. Read the statements below. Then listen and choose the right directions.

a. Go straight ahead for seven blocks and turn right. The hospital is on your right.
b. Go straight ahead for seven blocks and turn right. The hospital is on your left.
c. Go straight ahead for seven blocks and turn left. The hospital is on your left.

Can You Read a Map? Try this Test of Buenos Aires.

Imagine you're in Buenos Aires for the first time. It's the city of the tango and home to 10 million Argentines. You have your map and you're ready to go, but how are your map-reading skills? Can you follow directions, or do you get lost easily? Try this little test. As you read the descriptions below, find the places on the map.

1 Plaza de Mayo (May Plaza) This plaza or square is over 400 years old, and it is in the eastern part of the city near the river. Several important buildings are on this plaza including the Cabildo (the town hall) and the presidential palace, called the Casa Rosada (Pink House).

2 Avenida Florida (Florida Avenue) This street is only one block west of the Cabildo. It's probably the most popular shopping street in the city. There are over 600 shops here, and it is a pedestrian area. That means that people, not cars, travel up and down this street.

3 Avenida 9 de Julio (9th of July Avenue) Five blocks west of Florida is another famous Argentine street, Avenida 9 de Julio. It is one of the widest boulevards in the world. There are many interesting places here, including the obelisk and the 9 de Julio fountain.

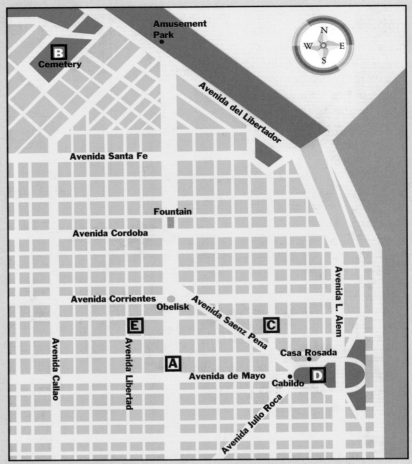

4 Teatro Colón (Columbus Theater) Two more blocks west of the obelisk is Avenida Libertad (Liberty Avenue) and the Teatro Colón, a famous opera house. Some of the best performers in the world sing here.

5 La Recoleta La Recoleta, about 15 blocks north from Teatro Colón, is a popular attraction for tourists. This historic neighborhood is famous for its cemetery. Many important Argentines are buried here, including Eva Perón. There are also many fashionable restaurants here and some of the most beautiful homes in Buenos Aires.

Solution
1. D
2. C
3. A
4. E
5. B

Imagine you and your friends have one day to see Buenos Aires. Working in groups of four, do the following:

1. Choose four places to visit.
2. Decide where to go first, second, third, and last.
3. Indicate your route on the map.

Review of units 1-4

1 ▶ Keiko Kurosawa is trying to find Alfredo Rivera at the International Business Association (IBA) conference in Honolulu. Complete their conversation.

Keiko Excuse me—are you Alfredo Rivera?
Alfredo —————— .
Keiko Hello, Mr. Rivera. I'm Keiko Kurosawa from Electronic Office News here in Honolulu.
Alfredo —————————————— .

▶ Working in groups of four, write the names on the right on four pieces of paper. Choose one piece of paper, but don't tell the group your name.
▶ Imagine you're at the IBA conference. Find the other three people and introduce yourself.

IBA CONFERENCE Keiko Kurosawa Electronic News	**IBA CONFERENCE** Mark Harper King Wire Service
IBA CONFERENCE Alfredo Rivera Global Computer	**IBA CONFERENCE** Cathy Marceau World Press

2 ▶ Mark Harper introduces Keiko to his friend Cathy Marceau. Complete Keiko's side of the conversation.
▶ In groups of three, act out the conversation using your own names and information.

Mark Hi, Keiko. How are you?
Keiko —————— . —————————— ?
Mark Fine. Keiko, this is my friend Cathy.
Keiko —————————————— .
Cathy Nice to meet you, too.
Keiko —————————————— ?
Cathy I'm from Ottawa, Canada.

▶ Say good-bye and end the conversation.

　　Cathy Good-bye, everyone.
Mark, Keiko —————— .
　　Cathy Nice meeting you, Keiko.
　　Keiko —————————————— .

 3 ▶ Listen to the conversation and complete Cathy's registration form below.
▶ Complete the last registration form for a classmate.

International Business Association	**International Business Association**	**International Business Association**
Name _Keiko Kurosawa_ **Address** _658 Kolopua Street_ _Honolulu, HI　96819_ _U.S.A._	**Name** _Cathy Marceau_ **Address** —————————— —————————— ——————————	**Name** —————————— **Address** —————————— —————————— ——————————

4 ► **Review the pronunciation of numbers. Practice the conversation using the addresses in the box.**

A What's your address?
B 113 First Avenue.
A One thirty or one thirteen?
B One thirteen.

113 First Avenue
770 Fifth Street
214 Third Street
1550 Tenth Avenue
319 Seventh Street

5 ► **Work in groups of three. Play these roles:**

Student A You're at the IBA conference and are trying to reach one of the people on the notepad. Make the two phone calls below.

Student B You answer the phone in conversation 1.

Student C You're the operator in conversation 2. Give Student A the correct phone numbers.

1. **A** (*Dials number*) *Rrring, rrring*
   B Hello?
   A _____ ?
   B I'm sorry. You have the wrong number.
   A _____ ?
   B Yes, it is, but I'm not Mary Harrison.
   A _____ .
   B That's O.K.

Harrison, Mary   555-3789
Herrera, Tomas   555-1739
Ho, Dae Jin   555-5433
Howell, Louise   555-9078
Hua, Lin   555-2861
Hunter, Susan   555-6652

2. **A** (*Dials number*) *Rrring, rrring*
   C Directory Assistance. May I help you?
   A _____ .
   C Is it in Honolulu?
   A _____ .
   C The number is _____ .
   A _____ .
   C You're welcome.

Haleamau, Loke 555-8920
Han, Chan Hee. 555-1641
Hanohano, Kaniela. 555-6651
Harrison, Mary. 555-3689
Herrera, Tomas. 555-1730
Ho, Dae Jin. 555-6433
Horbieta, Maria. 555-4358
Horvath, James. 555-1896
Howell, Louise. 555-9088
Hua, Lin. 555-2869
Hunter, Susan. 555-6651
Hutton, Joseph. 555-0444

6 ► **Act out the conversation in groups of three. Use your own information.**

A Hello?
B _____ ?
A Yes, he (she) is. Just a minute, please.
C _____ ?
A Hi, _____ . This is _____ .
C _____ ?
A Not bad. And you?
C _____ .

7 ► **Mark, Cathy, and Keiko are being interviewed on the evening news. Fill in the blanks with the correct forms of *be*. Use contractions if possible.**

Interviewer We _____ at the International Business Association conference here in Honolulu, and people _____ here from many countries. Where _____ you from? The United States?

Mark No, we _____ . We _____ from Ottawa, Canada. I _____ Mark Harper, and this _____ my colleague, Cathy Marceau.

Interviewer It _____ very nice to meet you. (*Turning to Keiko*) And you? Where _____ you from? _____ you from Canada, too?

Keiko Me? No, I _____ from Canada. I _____ from right here, Honolulu.

8 ▶ Work in small groups. Imagine that you and your classmates are in a snack bar. Offer to buy something for your classmates, using the questions in the box below.

Do you want some _____?
How about some _____?
Do you have change for _____?

coffee

soda

gum

CANDY

candy

popcorn

9A ▶ Student A follows the instructions below.
Student B follows the instructions on p. A44.

Student A You're at the telephone at the City Convention Center. Ask your partner for directions to the places in the box. Locate each building on the map below. Then use the map to give directions to the places your partner asks about.

Where is . . . ?

the Grand Hotel
the Holiday Disco
Brown's Record Store
the Town Library
Sam's Drugstore

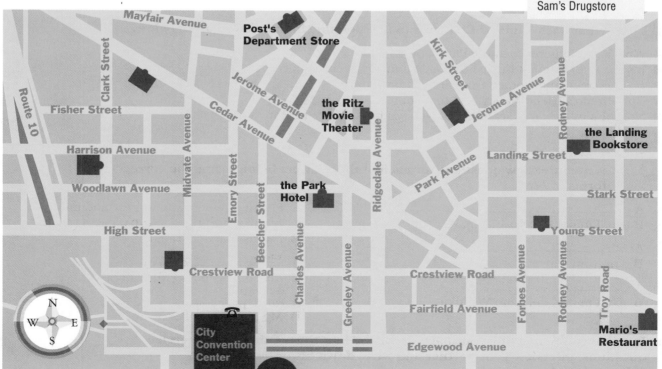

► **Student B follows the instructions below.**
Student A follows the instructions on p. A43.

Student B You're at the telephone at the City Convention Center. Use the map below to give directions to the places your partner asks about. Then ask your partner for directions to the places in the box. Locate each building on the map.

Where is . . . ?

Mario's Restaurant
the Park Hotel
Post's Department Store
the Landing Bookstore
the Ritz Movie Theater

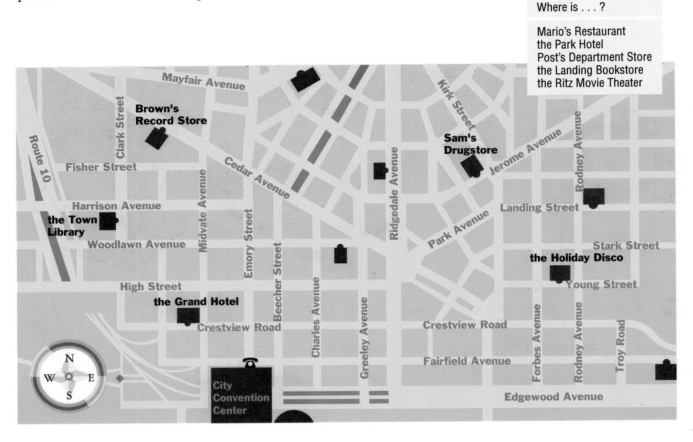

10 ► **What does 's mean? Change 's to is if possible in the conversation below.**

A What**'s** the conference at the Park Hotel?
B It**'s** the International Business Association conference—a conference for businessmen and women from around the world.
A Oh! Alfredo**'s** friend Nancy is at that conference.
B No, she**'s** in Italy on vacation, but Nancy**'s** boss is here in Honolulu for the conference.

11 ► **Write interview questions for each of the answers below, using the correct forms of be.**

1. **A** _____ ?
   B No, I'm not. I'm Toshi Tanaka.

2. **A** _____ ?
   B I'm from Hawaii.

3. **A** _____ ?
   B No, I'm not. I'm from Wailuku.

4. **A** Please give me your address and phone number. But first, _____ again?
   B My last name is Tanaka.

5. **A** _____ ?
   B My address is 213 Mailani Street.

6. **A** And _____ ?
   B My phone number at work is 555-3294.

► **Imagine you're meeting your partner for the first time. Using your interview questions, interview your partner and write down his or her answers.**
► **Tell another classmate about your partner.**

FUNCTIONS/THEMES	LANGUAGE	FORMS
Talk about jobs and occupations	Laura is an accountant. She works in an office. Accountants work in offices.	Formulaic use of the third person simple present: statements Articles *a* and *an* Plurals of nouns
Talk about your job	What do you do? I'm a doctor. Where do you work? I work at Memorial Hospital.	Simple present with *you* and *I*: statements; questions and short answers
Talk about where you live	Do you live around here? Do you live in an apartment/a house? Where do you live? On Maple Street./At 25 Maple Street./On the second floor./In apartment 2B.	Prepositions *in*, *on*, and *at*
Exchange personal information	Are you married? No, I'm single.	

Preview the conversations.

Kate sees Linda at a bus stop.
How do they greet each other?
Are they friends or acquaintances?

They're bowing.

They're shaking hands.

They're kissing.

They're hugging.

Here are some different ways of greeting people. How do you greet friends? Acquaintances? Family members? Do you bow, shake hands, kiss, hug, or just say "hello"?

26. Bus stop

Kate runs into Linda, an old acquaintance, at a bus stop.

A

Kate Linda!
Linda Kate! How are you?
Do you work around here?
Kate Yes, I work in that
building across the street.
Linda Really? What do you do?
Kate I'm a lawyer.
Linda Oh, that's interesting.
Kate What about you? What
do *you* do?
Linda I work at Memorial
Hospital.
Kate Oh . . . are you a doctor?
Linda No, I'm a biologist.
I do research.

B

Linda Here's my bus.
Kate That's my bus too.
Linda Oh, where do you live?
Kate On Grand Avenue.
Linda Really? Where on Grand?
Kate At 356.
Linda You're kidding! We're
neighbors. I live on the
next block.

C

Kate Do you live alone, Linda?
Linda No, I don't. I live with
my family. How about you?
Kate I'm married now. I got
married last year.
Linda Really? Congratulations!

Figure it out

**1. Listen to the conversation. What do
Kate and Linda do?**

1. Kate is a _____ .
2. Linda is a _____ .

2. Listen again. Say *true* or *false*.

1. Kate and Linda live on Grand Avenue. ✓
2. Kate and Linda live at 356 Grand Avenue. ✔
3. Linda lives alone. ●
4. Kate is married. ✓

3. Match.

1. What do you do?
2. Do you live around
   here?
3. Do you live alone?
4. I'm married now.
5. Where do you work?

a. No, I'm married.
b. I work across
   the street.
c. I'm a biologist.
d. No, I don't. I live
   on State Street.
e. Congratulations!

27. Jobs and occupations

1. David
teacher

2. Bill
mechanic

hospital

garage

3. Pedro
doctor

10. Noriko
banker

restaurant

office

4. Pravit
cook

9. Laura
accountant

school

bank

5. Jean
nurse

8. Barbara
secretary

7. Tom
waiter
(waitress: F)

6. Ana
lawyer

1 ► **What are the occupations of the people above? Where do they work?**

David is a teacher. He works in a school.

I	work
He/She	work**s**

Use **a** before a consonant sound: He's **a** teacher.

Use **an** before a vowel sound: She's **an** accountant.

2 ▶ Two of the people on p. A48 are talking. As you listen to their conversation, complete it below.
▶ Who are the two people? Identify A and B.

A What do you do?
B I'm _____ .
A Oh, really? Where do you work?
B _____ . How about you? What do you do?
A I'm _____ .

▶ Work in small groups and talk about what you do. Use personal information or choose an occupation from p. A48.

3 ▶ Using the information from exercise 2, introduce a student in your group to another classmate.

A _____ , this is _____ . _____ works at _____ .
B Oh, really? What do you do there?
C I'm _____ .

> Where do you work?
>
> **In** a hospital.
> **At** Memorial Hospital.

4 ▶ Study the frames: Plurals of Nouns

accountant	accountants	[s]

waiter	waiters	[z]
secretary	secretaries	
y: Change to i. Add -es.		

nurse	nurses	[ɪz]
waitress	waitresses	
ch, sh, s, z, x: Add -es.		

▶ Make a general statement about each occupation on p. A48.

Teachers work in schools.

5 ▶ Look at the three married couples. What are their jobs? Use the clues below.

Maria works in a hospital, but she's not a doctor.
Maria is a nurse.
Gloria works in a law office, but she's not a lawyer.
The nurse's husband works in a school.
The secretary is married to an accountant.
Ann works in an office, but it's not a doctor's office.
Mark works in an office, but it's not a law office.

doctor	nurse	teacher
accountant	secretary	lawyer

Carlos and Maria Madera

Mark and Ann Gardner

Martin and Gloria Jacobson

28. Where do you live?

TALK ABOUT WHERE YOU LIVE

1 ► Complete the conversations below with appropriate questions from the box.
► Listen to check your answers.
► Practice the conversations with a partner, using personal information.

> Where do you live? Do you live around here? How about you?
> What floor? Where on Maple Street?

1. **A** _____ ?
   B In Tokyo.
   _____ ?
   A I live in Bangkok.

2. **A** _____ ?
   B Yes, I live on Maple Street.
   A Really? _____ ?
   B At 25—between Main and Ridge.
   A Oh, we're neighbors! I live on the same block.

3. **A** _____ ?
   B Two, please.

> **in** Bangkok   **on** Maple Street   **at** 25 Maple Street
> **in** Apartment 2B   **on** the second floor

2 ► Look at the picture below and think about the situation.
► Working in groups of six, find out where your classmates live.
► Two classmates have cars. Decide who will go home in each of the two cars.

29. How about you?

1 ▶ **Study the frames: Simple Present with *I* and *You***

Information questions			
Where	**do**	you	**live?** **work?**

Affirmative statements		
I	**live** **work**	on Maple Street.

Negative statements			
I	**don't**	**live** **have**	around here. a job.

Yes-no questions			
Do	you	**live** **work**	around here?

Short answers		
Yes,	I	**do.**
No,		**don't.**

Compare the present of *be* and the simple present:
Are you married? Yes, I **am**.
Do you **live** around here? Yes, I **do**.

2 ▶ **Working in small groups, write interview questions for each of the answers below.**

1. _____ ?
   Yes, I live on this block.

2. _____ ?
   No, I live in a house.

3. _____ ?
   No, I don't. I live with my family.

4. _____ ?
   No, I'm single.

5. _____ ?
   I'm an accountant.

6. _____ ?
   I work at the Playful Toy Company on Main Street.

Do you live alone?
No, I'm married.

Do you live in an apartment?
Yes, I do.

Do you live alone?
Yes, I'm single.

▶ **Using your interview questions, interview four classmates. Write down their answers.**

▶ **Act out one of your interviews for other classmates.**

30. Cafeteria

Carolyn runs into Maggie in a cafeteria. Maggie is on her lunch hour.

1

Carolyn	Hi, Maggie!
Maggie	Carolyn! Nice to see you. Have a seat.
Carolyn	Thanks.
Maggie	How are you doing?
Carolyn	Fine. How about you?
Maggie	Oh, I'm fine, thanks.
Carolyn	Do you work around here?
Maggie	Yes, I work at Brooklyn Hospital.
Carolyn	Oh, what kind of work do you do?
Maggie	I'm a lab technician.
Carolyn	Hmm . . . that sounds interesting.
Maggie	Yes, it's a good job. What do *you* do?
Carolyn	Me? Oh, I'm an actress.
Maggie	Really? How exciting!
Carolyn	Well . . . I'm out of work.
Maggie	Oh, that's not so exciting.
Carolyn	No, it isn't. Right now, I'm looking for an office job.
Maggie	Well, I hope you find something. Anyway . . . speaking of work, I've got to get back to the hospital. See you later.
Carolyn	Bye.

2. Figure it out

1. *True* or *False*? Correct the false statements.

1. Maggie works in a hospital.
2. Maggie is a doctor.
3. Carolyn is an actress.
4. Maggie has a good job.
5. Carolyn has a good job.

2. Find another way to say it.

1. How are you? *How are you doing?*
2. I don't have a job.
3. Do you work in the neighborhood?
4. Sit down.
5. What do you do?

📼 3. Listen in

Irma, the woman on the left, runs into an old acquaintance, Joe. Read the statements. Then listen to the conversation and choose *a*, *b*, or *c*.

1. _____ is a lawyer.
   a. Irma
   b. Joe
   c. Bill Evans

2. Irma _____ .
   a. lives alone
   b. lives with Bill
   c. lives with a friend

📼 4. How to say it

Listen to these questions about jobs.

1. <u>Where do you</u> work? [ˈwerdəyu]
2. <u>What do you</u> do? [ˈwədəyu]
3. <u>Is he</u> a doctor? [ˈɪzi]
4. <u>Is she</u> a lawyer? [ˈɪʃi]

5. Your turn

Sam, the man on the left, is having lunch with an old acquaintance, Judy. What do you think he is saying? Complete Sam's part of the conversation. Then act out the conversation with a partner.

Sam So, how's everything?
Judy Good. How are things with you?
Sam Not bad. _____?
Judy Yes, I work down the street. How about you? Where do you work?
Sam _____ .
Judy Really? What do you do there?
Sam _____ .
Judy Oh, that's interesting. Do you live near here, too?
Sam _____ .
Judy You're kidding! My sister lives across the street from you.

31. How do you like your job?

Richard Daniels, clown
I really enjoy my job. I like to laugh and I love people, especially children. I can also travel a lot.

Pete Bennett, sanitation worker
I don't really like my job, but what else can I do? I have a family, and we need the money.

Sandy Jackson, park ranger
I love my job. I work outside most of the day. I like the outdoors a lot, so I feel I'm very lucky. I do a job I enjoy.

Eloida Jaico, accountant
Well, it's a job that I do well. It pays well too, but sometimes I think I'd like to do something a little more exciting.

Manuel Rivas, veterinarian's assistant
I like my job just fine. It's only a part-time job now, but I'd like to get more experience and make it a full-time job.

Clifford Hall, police officer
Sometimes I like my job, and other times I hate it. My wife doesn't like it at all. She thinks it's dangerous. But the work is important.

Read the article. Then answer the questions.

1. Which people like their jobs?
2. Which people aren't sure that they like their jobs?
3. Which people don't like their jobs?
4. Who is married, according to the article?
5. Who likes children, according to the article?

FUNCTIONS/THEMES	LANGUAGE	FORMS
Give day, month, and year Talk about birthdays and birth dates	What's the date next Sunday? It's February twelfth (12th). When's your birthday? It's January thirty-first (31st). What year were you born? In nineteen seventy-one (1971).	Ordinal numbers 11th–31st Formulaic use of *was* and *were* with *born*
Give information about people	Christine Pappas lives at 27 Willow Street. She goes to high school and she works at Macy's.	Simple present: affirmative statements; irregular verbs; third person singular pronunciation
Talk about family	Samuel and Nancy are husband and wife. Do you have any brothers or sisters? What does your sister do?	Terminology for family relationships Summary of simple present: questions, statements, and short answers
Talk about languages and nationalities	What language do they speak in Jamaica? Do you speak Portuguese? Are you Brazilian?	More simple present
Ask what something means Ask how to say something Ask for clarification	What does *mucho gusto* mean? It means "Nice to meet you." How do you say "thank you" in Korean? Excuse me? Could you speak a little slower, please?	More simple present
Ask to borrow something	Could I use your pencil? Sure, here.	Formula *Could I . . . ?*

Preview the conversations.

Ellen and Lisa don't know each other, but they are talking together on the plane. Do you like to talk to strangers on planes?

Visitors to the United States fill out this form when they arrive. What do visitors to your country have to do?

UNIT 6 • LESSONS 32–38

32. Vacation

Lisa Chou meets Ellen Stone on a flight from Taipei to New York.

Flight attendant Take this form, fill it out, and keep it with your passport. You'll need it to pass through Immigration.

Lisa I'm sorry, could you speak a little slower, please?

Flight attendant Oh, sure. Fill out this form and keep it with your passport. *(To Lisa's husband)* Here's one for you, too.

Lisa He doesn't speak English.

Flight attendant Could you help him?

Lisa Sure.

Lisa Excuse me—what does "city where you boarded" mean?

Ellen It means the city where you got on the plane.

Lisa Thanks. And one more thing—what does "birth date" mean?

Ellen It's the month, day, and year you were born.

Lisa Oh, I see. Thank you.

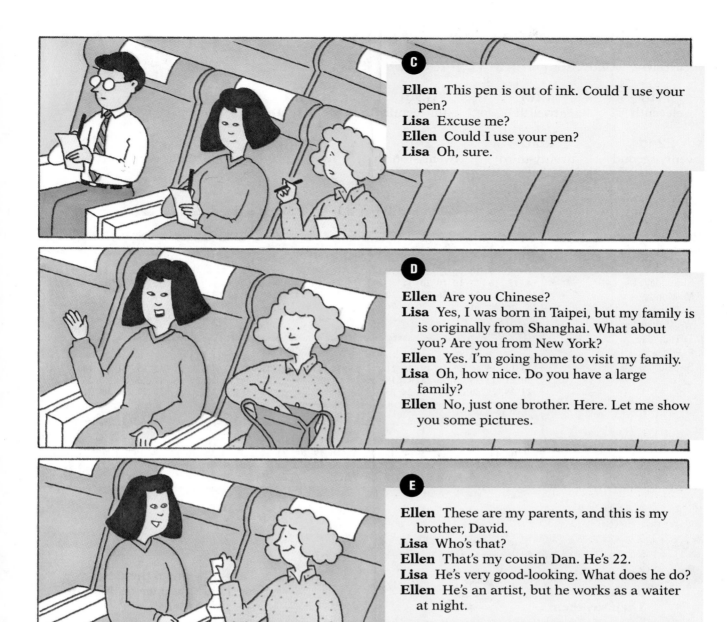

C

Ellen This pen is out of ink. Could I use your pen?
Lisa Excuse me?
Ellen Could I use your pen?
Lisa Oh, sure.

D

Ellen Are you Chinese?
Lisa Yes, I was born in Taipei, but my family is is originally from Shanghai. What about you? Are you from New York?
Ellen Yes. I'm going home to visit my family.
Lisa Oh, how nice. Do you have a large family?
Ellen No, just one brother. Here. Let me show you some pictures.

E

Ellen These are my parents, and this is my brother, David.
Lisa Who's that?
Ellen That's my cousin Dan. He's 22.
Lisa He's very good-looking. What does he do?
Ellen He's an artist, but he works as a waiter at night.

Figure it out

1. Listen to the conversations and answer the questions.

1. Where is Lisa from?
2. Where is Ellen from?

2. Listen again. Say *true, false,* or *it doesn't say*.

1. Lisa's husband speaks English. F 2
2. Ellen's family lives in New York. T 1
3. Ellen's cousin is a cook. 3
4. Lisa and her husband have friends in New York. F 2
5. Ellen is a student. 3

3. Match the items on the Arrival Record on p. A56.

1. Family name
2. First name
3. Sex
4. Date issued
5. Country of citizenship
6. City where you boarded
7. Address while in the United States

a. 23 Lexington Avenue
b. Chou
c. Lisa
d. Taiwan
e. female
f. Taipei
g. May 23, 1990

33. When's your birthday?

11th	**12th**	**13th**	**14th**	**20th**	**21st**
eleventh	twelfth	thirteenth	fourteenth	twentieth	twenty-first
22nd	**23rd**	**24th**	**25th**	**30th**	**31st**
twenty-second	twenty-third	twenty-fourth	twenty-fifth	thirtieth	thirty-first

1 ▶ **Say the dates in blue on the calendar. What day is it? What's the date?**

It's Thursday, January 11th.

S=Sunday
M=Monday
T=Tuesday
W=Wednesday
T=Thursday
F=Friday
S=Saturday

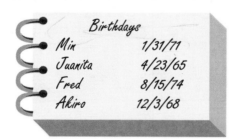

[Calendar showing months JANUARY through DECEMBER]

DATES

2 ▶ **Listen to the dates on the notepad. Then say them.**

1/31/71 is said
"January thirty-first,
nineteen seventy-one."

Birthdays

Min	1/31/71
Juanita	4/23/65
Fred	8/15/74
Akiro	12/3/68

▶ **Write down the dates you hear. Then write them in short form.**

1. *December 4, 1982 (12/4/82)*
2. _____
3. _____
4. _____
5. _____

3 ▶ **Ask a partner questions like these. He or she will answer using a calendar.**

1. What's today's date? *January 11th.*
2. What day is today? *Thursday.*
3. What's the date tomorrow?
4. What's the date next Sunday?

TALK ABOUT BIRTHDAYS

4 ▶ **Listen to the conversation and complete it.**

A When's your birthday?
B _____ .
A What year were you born?
B _____ .

▶ **Try to find another student who . . .**

1. . . . was born the same month as you.
2. . . . was born the same day of the week as you.
3. . . . has the same birthday as you.
4. . . . was born the same year as you.
5. . . . has the same birth date as you.

34. Family tree

FAMILY MEMBERS

1 ► Look at Barbara Butler's family tree and the pictures below.
Say how the people in the pictures are related.

Samuel and Nancy are husband and wife.

The Butler Family

1. husband   wife

2. mother   daughter

3. father   son

4. uncle   nephew

5. aunt   niece

6. grandfather   grandson

7. grandmother   granddaughter

8. sister   brother

9. cousins

2 ► Fill in the blanks with the correct words.

1. Charles' wife is Samuel's _*mother*_ .
2. Jack's sister is Tim's _Daughter_
3. Lynn's father is Lily's _Husband_
4. Judy's mother is Tim's _Wife_
5. Nancy's son is Barbara's _Brother_

6. Rick's grandfather is Samuel's _father_ .
7. Tim's wife is Rick's _Aunt_
8. Samuel's mother is Barbara's _Grandmother_
9. Judy's father is Barbara's _uncle_
10. Lynn's daughter is Samuel's _Niece_

3 ► Who's talking? Listen to some members of Barbara's family describe themselves. Identify the speakers.

1. _Barbara_   3. _Jack_   5. _Lily_
2. _Nancy_   4. _Samuel_   6. _Tim_

4 ► Draw your own family tree. Use Barbara Butler's tree as a model.

35. Who's that?

Christine Pappas

I live with my parents at 27 Willow Street. I go to high school, and I have a job, too. I work at Macy's Department Store in the evenings. My parents own a grocery store.

Jeff Hunt

I live with my parents at 93 Pineapple Street. I work at Arno's Coffee Shop. My parents teach at Brooklyn College. My mother teaches biology, and my father teaches English.

George Arno

I live at 5 Willow Street. I own Arno's Coffee Shop with my wife, Loretta. I work there all day and I really enjoy my work. I meet many interesting people there.

Maggie Sloane

I live at 3 Willow Street. I live alone and I really like my apartment. I'm a lab technician at Brooklyn Hospital.

  1 ▶ **Listen to the information above about some people at Arno's Coffee Shop.**
▶ **Say where each person lives and works.**

A Who's that?
B Oh, that's Christine Pappas. She lives at 27 Willow Street.
A Where does she work?
B She works at Macy's.

| I live |
| He/She live**s** |

---

 2 ▶ **Study the frames: Simple Present**

Regular verbs		
I You We They	work live teach	in Brooklyn.
He She	work**s** live**s** teach**es**	

Pronunciation	
work**s**	[s]
live**s**	[z]
teach**es**	[ɪz]

Irregular verbs	
I **have** a sister.	He **has** a sister.
We **go** to school.	She **goes** to school.
They **do** homework.	He **does** homework.

▶ **Listen to the sentences in the frame that begin with *he* and *she*. Notice the pronunciation of the third person forms of the verbs.**

3 ▶ **Work in groups of four. Choose one of the people above and study carefully the information under the picture.**
▶ **Tell the classmates in your group everything you can remember about the person. (Try not to look in your book.)**

Christine Pappas lives with her parents at 27 Willow Street. She goes to high school and . . .

| he → his |
| she → her |

4 ▶ **Study the frames: Simple Present**

Information questions				Statements		
Where	**do**	you they	**work**?	I We They	**work** **don't work**	here.
	does	he she		He She	**works** **doesn't work**	

Yes-no questions				Short answers		
Do	you they	**work** here?		Yes,	I we they	**do.**
				No,		**don't.**
Does	he she			Yes,	he	**does.**
				No,	she	**doesn't.**

5 ▶ **Ask an appropriate question about Christine Pappas for each of the answers below.**
▶ **Ask similar questions about the other people on p. A60. Your partner will try to answer from memory.**

1. **A** _____ ?
   B She lives at 27 Willow Street.

2. **A** _____ ?
   B No, she doesn't. She lives with her parents.

3. **A** _____ ?
   B Yes, she does. She works at Macy's Department Store.

4. **A** _____ ?
   B They own a grocery store.

6 ▶ **Some friends are looking at photos. Listen to the conversation.**

A Who's that?
B Oh, that's my sister, Carla.
A She's very pretty. How old is she?
B Twenty-four.
A What does she do?
B She's an accountant. She works in a bank.

> man: good-looking, handsome
> woman: good-looking, pretty
> child: good-looking, cute

▶ **Bring to class photos of family members and friends.**
▶ **Show your pictures to a partner and talk about the people in them.**

7 ▶ **Interview three classmates about their families and record their answers. Ask questions like the ones below.**
▶ **Tell the rest of the class about one classmate and his or her family.**

1. Do you live with your parents?
2. Do you have any brothers and sisters?
3. What are their names?
4. What do they do?
5. Do you have any nieces and nephews?

> they → their

6. Are you married?
7. What does your husband/wife do?
8. Do you have any children? How old are they?
9. Do you have a lot of family (*cousins, aunts uncles*) in (*name of city*)?

36. Do you speak Chinese?

See p. A86 for a more complete list of languages, countries, and nationalities.

1 ▶ **Look at the chart of some common languages and answer the questions.**

1. What language do they speak in Jamaica?
2. What are two languages they speak in India?
3. What language do they speak in Chile?
4. What language do Brazilians speak?
5. Where do they speak Arabic?
6. Where do they speak Chinese?

Languages	Countries	Nationalities
Chinese	China ✓	Chinese ✓
English	the United Kingdom the United States Jamaica ✓	British American Jamaican ✓
Spanish	Spain Mexico Chile	Spanish Mexican Chilean
Hindi	India	Indian
Bengali	Bangladesh India	Bangladeshi Indian
Arabic	Morocco Jordan Saudi Arabia	Moroccan Jordanian Saudi Arabian
Japanese	Japan	Japanese
German	Germany Switzerland Austria	German Swiss Austrian
Portuguese	Portugal Brazil	Portuguese

 2 ▶ **Complete the conversations below. Then listen to confirm your answers.**

1. **A** Do you speak _____ ?
   B Yes, I do.
   A Are you British?
   B No, I'm _____ .

2. **A** Where are you from?
   B I'm from _____ .
   A Oh, do you speak Hindi?
   B No, I speak _____ .

3 ▶ **Imagine that you're from one of the countries in the chart. Write down your new language and nationality on a piece of paper.**
▶ **Find out other students' new languages and nationalities. Find someone who . . .**

1. . . . is Chinese and speaks Chinese.
2. . . . is Indian, but doesn't speak Bengali.
3. . . . speaks English, but isn't from the United States.
4. . . . speaks Portuguese, but isn't Brazilian.
5. . . . speaks Spanish, but isn't Spanish.
6. . . . is Japanese and speaks Japanese.
7. . . . speaks Arabic, but isn't from Jordan.
8. . . . speaks German, but isn't from Germany.

4 ► Look at the foreign expressions in the box below. Find out what they mean. (You may find the answers on p. A87.)

A Do you speak Spanish?
B Yes, I do.
A What does *mucho gusto* mean?
B (It means) "Nice to meet you."

Some foreign expressions

Mucho gusto. (Spanish)   Do svidanye. (Russian)
Shukran. (Arabic)   Habari gani. (Swahili)
Parakalo. (Greek)   Arigato. (Japanese)
Obrigado. (Portuguese)   Pen yangai. (Thai)

5 ► Find out how to say each English expression below in two languages.

A Do you speak Korean?
B A little.
A How do you say "thank you" in Korean?
B *Kamsamida*.

Some English expressions

Thank you.   Good-bye.
Hello.   I love you.
Please.   How are you?

6 ► Match each question with another way to say it.

1. What's your address?
2. What's your date of birth?
3. What's your place of birth?
4. What's your marital status?
5. What's your place of employment?
6. What's your business phone?

a. Are you married or single?
b. Where were you born?
c. Where do you live?
d. When were you born?
e. What's your phone number at work?
f. Where do you work?

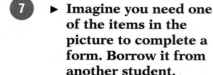

► Listen to the conversation below.
► Copy the form and fill it out for another student.

A What's your date of birth?
B Excuse me?
A When were you born?
B September 15, 1965.
A Could you speak a little slower, please?
B Oh, sure. September 15, 1965.

GLOBAL BANK
VISTA CARD APPLICATION

Please fill out the form below to apply for your Global Bank Vista Card.

PERSONAL INFORMATION

Name
  Ann Robards
Address
  1422 Chadwick Drive, Dayton, Ohio 45406
Date of Birth   Place of Birth
  |0|9|1|5|6|5| *Lima, Peru*
Marital Status
  Married

EMPLOYMENT INFORMATION

Place of Employment
  Fairview High School
Address
  16 Main Street, Dayton, Ohio
Business Phone
  513-555-3331

7 ► Imagine you need one of the items in the picture to complete a form. Borrow it from another student.

A Excuse me, do you have a pencil?
B No, I'm sorry, I don't.

A Excuse me, could I use your pencil?
C Sure, here.
A Thanks.

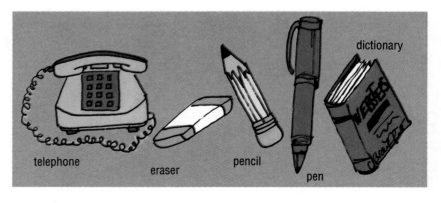

telephone   eraser   pencil   pen   dictionary

37. Take my advice.

John Pierce is watching TV one evening when Mrs. Baxter knocks at the door.

(1)

Mrs. Baxter	(*Knock, knock, knock!*)
John	Who is it?
Mrs. Baxter	It's Mrs. Baxter.
John	(*To himself*) Mrs. Baxter? (*Opening the door*) Mrs. Baxter! How are you this evening?
Mrs. Baxter	Good evening, Mr. Pierce. I'm sorry to bother you.
John	Oh, that's O.K. I was just watching television. Come in. Sit down. Would you like . . . uh . . . some tea? Or coffee?
Mrs. Baxter	Oh, no, please don't bother. I only have a few minutes. Uh, Mr. Pierce . . . it's the fourth of December.
John	The fourth of . . . oh, Mrs. Baxter, the rent! I'm sorry it's late. I'll write you a check right now. Uh . . . do you have a pen I could use?
Mrs. Baxter	Yes, I do. Here you are.

Mrs. Baxter	Is that your girlfriend?
John	My girlfriend? Oh, you mean in the picture. No, that's my sister.
Mrs. Baxter	She's very pretty. Is she married?
John	Yes, married with two children—a boy and a girl.
Mrs. Baxter	Oh, how wonderful!
John	Do you have any children, Mrs. Baxter?
Mrs. Baxter	Mr. Pierce, I have six grandchildren!
John	Oh, really? (*Handing her the check*) Here you are, Mrs. Baxter.
Mrs. Baxter	Do you have a girlfriend?
John	No, not really.
Mrs. Baxter	What? A handsome man like you with a good job? Take my advice. Find yourself a girlfriend, get married, and have children. (*Rrring, rrring*)
John	Oh, there's the phone. Excuse me for just one moment, Mrs. Baxter . . .

2. Figure it out

1. *True* or *False*?

1. John's rent check is late.
2. John has a girlfriend.
3. Mrs. Baxter has no children.
4. Mrs. Baxter's advice is, "Get married and have children."
5. John is happy to listen to Mrs. Baxter's advice.

2. What do you think? Does Mrs. Baxter have good advice?

3. Listen in

John forgets to meet his friend Gloria.
Read the statements below. Then listen to the conversation and complete them.

1. The House of China is at 352 _____ Avenue.
2. Gloria's birthday is _____ .

4. Your turn

Arnold Schwarzenegger is interviewed on television. Act out a conversation between him and the interviewer. Use this information:

Arnold Schwarzenegger is from Austria.
He lives in California now.
He speaks German and English.
He's an actor and a businessman.

5. How to say it

Listen to the conversations.

1. **A** My brother is 22.
   B <u>Does he</u> live at home?   ['dəzi]
   A No, he lives with friends.
   B <u>What does he</u> do?   ['wədəzi]
   A He's an actor.

2. **A** My sister is 24.
   B <u>Does she</u> live with you?   ['dəʃi]
   A No, she's married.
   B <u>What does she</u> do?   ['wədəʃi]
   A She's a doctor.

38.

SO YOU WANT TO LEARN ENGLISH ... *FAST!*

You need to improve your English for work or travel. **You want to practice your language skills, but you don't have the opportunity. What do you do?**

Learn the IST way! Take a "study vacation" and travel to English-speaking countries.

With IST, International Student Travel, you can spend one to three months abroad improving your speaking, listening, reading and writing skills. Live with an English-speaking family. During the day, study full time in a high school or language institute. The choice is yours!

Where can you go? The United States and England are very popular for study holidays. Canada is another choice. And don't forget Australia and New Zealand, two more countries where people speak English. Each can provide you with the experience of a lifetime.

Enjoy the sights and learn English in Sydney.

London is an interesting place to study English.

Take a "Study Vacation" to Washington, D.C.

- -

INTERNATIONAL STUDENT TRAVEL
500 Fifth Avenue, 4th Floor
New York, NY   10020
U.S.A.

Yes! Please send me more information about opportunities to study in English-speaking countries.

Name _____

Address _____
    Street and Number
_____
    City   **State**   **Zip Code**
_____
    Country

IST offers tours, short courses, and full-time study opportunities. For more information call us now at 1-800-555-2700 or send in the coupon.

INTERNATIONAL STUDENT TRAVEL can help you achieve your goals!

---

1. Read the advertisement. Then scan it again and find . . .

1. . . . five countries where you can learn English.
2. . . . three cities where you can study English with International Student Travel.
3. . . . another way to say "language school."
4. . . . the abbreviation for International Student Travel.
5. . . . the telephone number and address for International Student Travel.

2. What are two ways that you can get more information about International Student Travel?

PREVIEW

FUNCTIONS/THEMES	LANGUAGE	FORMS
Make a business telephone call Leave a message	May I help you? May I speak to Richard Lightner, please? May I take a message? Could you ask him to call me? I'll give him the message.	Formulas *May I . . . ?* and *I'll . . .* Object pronouns

Say hello and good-bye	Good morning/afternoon/evening.
	  Good-bye./Good night./Have a nice
	  weekend./See you tomorrow.	

Talk about leisure plans	What are you going to do this weekend?
	I'm going to visit a friend.
	What is Rob going to do tonight/
	  tomorrow evening/next weekend/on
	  Sunday?
		Formulaic use of future with
		  going to
		Expressions of future time

Preview the conversations.

Good morning, Martin and Brown. May I help you?

This is Bob Rosansky. May I speak to Laura Martin, please?

Laura, do you want to speak to Bob Rosansky?

No, Melissa, not until Monday.

I'm sorry, Mr. Rosansky. She's busy right now.

Notice how this receptionist answers the phone. How do receptionists answer the phone in your country?

The receptionist calls Bob Rosansky "Mr. Rosansky." She calls her boss "Laura." Does Laura Martin call her receptionist by her first name? When do you use first names in your country?

39. Friday

 It's a busy day for Melissa Harris, the receptionist at the law office of Laura Martin and Louis Brown.

A

Melissa Good morning, Martin and Brown. May I help you?

Bob Rosansky Yes. This is Bob Rosansky. May I speak to Laura Martin, please?

Melissa One moment, please. (*to Laura*) Do you want to speak to Bob Rosansky?

Laura No, Melissa. Not until Monday.

Melissa I'm sorry, Mr. Rosansky. She's busy right now. May I take a message?

Bob Rosansky Yes, could you ask her to call my office? My number there is 555-3492.

Melissa I'm sorry, could you repeat that?

Bob Rosansky 555-3492.

Melissa I'll give her the message.

B

Melissa Good afternoon, Martin and Brown. May I help you?

Bob Rosansky May I speak to Laura Martin or Louis Brown, please?

Melissa Who's calling, please?

Bob Rosansky Bob Rosansky.

Melissa I'm sorry. They're in a meeting right now. Can I give them a message, Mr. Rosansky?

Bob Rosansky No, I'll call back later.

C

Melissa Good afternoon, Martin and Brown. May I help you?

Bob Rosansky May I speak to Laura, please?

Melissa Who's calling, please?

Bob Rosansky Uh . . . it's her friend Bob.

Melissa Laura, your friend Bob is on the phone.

Laura Oh, thanks. Hi, Bob. How are you?

Bob Rosansky Ms. Martin? This is Bob Rosansky . . .

D

Melissa Good night, Louis. Good night, Laura. See you tomorrow.
Laura Tomorrow?
Melissa Wait a minute—what day is today?
Louis Friday.
Melissa Oh, yes—you're right.
Laura Have a nice weekend, Melissa.
Louis Yeah. Get some rest.
Melissa Thanks.

E

Laura What are you going to do this weekend, Louis?
Louis Oh, I don't have any plans. I'm just going to take it easy. What about you?
Laura I'd like to go to the beach, but I guess I'm going to work on that contract for Bob Rosansky. He wants it on Monday morning.
Louis Well, have fun.
Laura You too. See you Monday.

Figure it out

1. Listen to the conversations and answer the questions.

1. Does Laura Martin want to speak with Bob Rosansky? *No, she doesn't.*
2. Are Laura and Louis really in a meeting?
3. Does Bob Rosansky finally talk to Laura?
4. Does Melissa work on Saturday?
5. Does Louis have plans for the weekend?
6. Does Laura have plans for the weekend?

2. Listen again. Complete the sentences with *a*, *b*, or *c*.

1. In conversations A and B, Bob Rosansky identifies himself by his __*b*__ . When he asks to speak to Laura Martin, he uses her _____ .
2. When Melissa, the receptionist, speaks to Bob Rosansky, she uses his _____ .
3. In conversation C, Bob Rosansky identifies himself by his _____ . When he asks to speak to Laura Martin, he uses her _____ . When he finally speaks to Laura Martin, he uses her _____ .
4. When Melissa speaks to Laura Martin, she uses her _____ . When she speaks to Louis Brown, she uses his _____ . When the two lawyers speak to the receptionist, they use her _____ .

a. first name
b. first and last names
c. title and last name

3. Match.

1. Could you repeat your number, please?
2. Have a nice weekend.
3. Good night.
4. Good morning.
5. May I speak to Laura Martin, please?
6. May I take a message?

a. She's in a meeting right now.
b. See you tomorrow.
c. It's 555-3492.
d. No, I'll call back later.
e. You too. See you Monday.
f. Hello. How are you today?

40. May I take a message?

 1
- ▶ Listen to the two possible business calls below.
- ▶ Act out the calls with a partner. Call Global Travel in the afternoon and ask to speak to a classmate. Then call back in the evening.

A (Dials number) Rrring, rrring

B Good morning, Global Travel. May I help you?

A May I speak to Richard Lightner, please?

B I'm sorry, he isn't here right now.   **B** Just a moment, please.

A Thank you. I'll call back later.   **A** Thank you.

morning   afternoon   evening

 2
- ▶ Listen and complete the message with the caller's last name and telephone number.

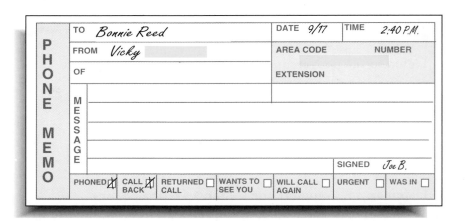

P H O N E   M E M O

TO	Bonnie Reed		DATE 9/17	TIME 2:40 P.M.
FROM	Vicky		AREA CODE	NUMBER
OF			EXTENSION	

M E S S A G E

SIGNED Joe B.

| PHONED ☒ | CALL BACK ☒ | RETURNED CALL ☐ | WANTS TO SEE YOU ☐ | WILL CALL AGAIN ☐ | URGENT ☐ | WAS IN ☐ |

 3
- ▶ Complete the conversation below with the sentences in the box.
- ▶ Listen to confirm your answers.
- ▶ Act out the conversation. Ask to speak to a classmate and substitute your own name for Rob Vale.

Receptionist _____

Rob Vale May I speak to Mrs. Reed, please?

Receptionist _____

Rob Vale Yes. This is Rob Vale. Could you ask her to call me?

Receptionist _____

Rob Vale "V" as in "Victor"—A-L-E.

Receptionist _____

Rob Vale No, she doesn't. It's 555-2811.

Receptionist _____

Rob Vale Thank you.

Mrs. Reed = her
Rob Vale = him

Certainly. Could you spell your last name, please?
I'll give her the message.
Does she have your number?
Global Travel. May I help you?
She isn't here right now. May I take a message?

Some difficult sounds

"V" as in "Victor"   "R" as in "Robert"
"B" as in "boy"   "S" as in "Sally"
"L" as in "Linda"   "F" as in "Frank"

4 ▶ **Brian calls his friend Liz at work. Then he calls her at home. To find the two conversations, choose *home* or *work* for each line below.**
▶ **Listen to confirm your answers.**

<u>home</u> **A** Hello?
<u>work</u> **A** Good morning. May I help you?

_____ **B** Yes. May I speak to Ms. McCann, please?
_____ **B** Hi. Is Liz there?

_____ **A** I'm sorry, she isn't here right now. Can I take a message?
_____ **A** I'm sorry, Ms. McCann isn't here right now. May I take a message?

_____ **B** Yeah. Could you ask her to call Brian?
_____ **B** Yes. Could you ask her to call Brian Dunn, please?

_____ **A** Certainly. Does she have your number, Mr. Dunn?
_____ **A** Sure. What's your number?

_____ **B** 555-2592.
_____ **B** No, she doesn't. It's 555-2592.

_____ **A** I'll give her the message.
_____ **A** O.K. I'll tell her.

_____ **B** Thank you. Good-bye.
_____ **B** Thanks. Bye.

MESSAGE	DATE <u>12/13/95</u>	TIME <u>3:10</u>
TO	<u>Ms. McCann</u>	
CALLER	<u>Brian Dunn</u>	
COMPANY	<u>Ace Computer</u>	
PHONE NUMBER	<u>555-2592</u>	

Please call today.

Liz,   12/13/95
Call Brian at 555-2592.

May I speak to . . . ? is formal.
Can I speak to . . . ? is less formal.
Is . . . there? is informal.

▶ **Act out the conversations with a partner. Ask to speak to someone of your choice.**
▶ **Take messages like the ones above.**

5 ▶ **Study the frame: Object Pronouns**

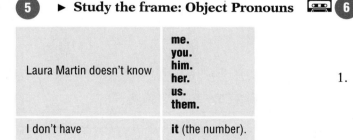

Laura Martin doesn't know	me. you. him. her. us. them.
I don't have	**it** (the number).

 6 ▶ **Complete the conversations below with object pronouns.**
▶ **Listen to the conversations to check your answers.**

1. **A** Can I speak to Nina Janik, please?
   B Nina isn't here right now. Can I give <u>*her*</u> a message?
   A Well, Nina doesn't know _____ . My name is Marcella. I have a message from her sister in Prague.

2. **A** Hi, Suzy. Are your parents home?
   B No, they aren't.
   A Well, could you ask _____ to call _____ tonight? This is Mrs. Fox.
   B Sure. I'll tell _____ . Oh, what's your number?
   A I think they have _____ , but it's 555-6679.

41. Have a nice weekend!

1 ▶ **Match the activities below with the pictures.**
▶ **Working in groups, make a list of your classmates' leisure-time activities.**

1. go to the movies *c*
2. visit my parents
3. read a good book
4. watch TV

5. do my homework
6. go to the beach
7. go to the country
8. take it easy

9. play tennis
10. have dinner with friends

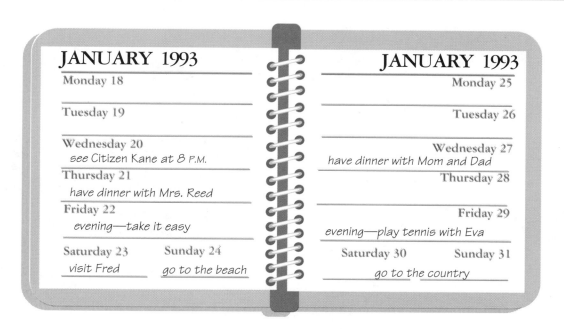

  2 ▶ Look at Rob Vale's calendar as you listen to his conversation below.
▶ Act out the conversation using personal information. Find out what two classmates are going to do this weekend.

Rob What are you going to do this weekend?
Amy I don't have any plans. What about you?
Rob On Saturday, I'm going to visit a friend.
And on Sunday, I'm going to go to the beach.
Amy Well, have a good time.
Rob Thanks. See you Monday.
Amy Bye.

Some ways to say good-bye
Good-bye. (Bye.) Have a good time.
Good night.   See you Monday.

Good night means **good-bye** and is used any time after the end of the work day.

3 ▶ Imagine that today is Wednesday. Answer questions 1-3 about Rob Vale.
Then ask similar questions using the expressions of future time in items 4-6.

1. What is Rob going to do tonight?
   He's going to see Citizen Kane.

2. What is he going to do tomorrow evening?
3. What is he going to do Friday evening?
4. . . . this weekend?
5. . . . next Wednesday?
6. . . . next weekend?

Some expressions of future time	
today	tomorrow
tonight	tomorrow night
this morning	tomorrow morning
this afternoon	tomorrow afternoon
this evening	tomorrow evening
this weekend	next weekend
on Saturday/Sunday/Monday . . .	

▶ Make your own calendar for this week and next week.
▶ Using the expressions of future time in the box, find out three classmates' plans for this week and next week.

42. Win a trip for two.

On a cold day in New York, George enters a contest for a trip to Florida. Then he runs into his friend Nick.

1. How to say it

Listen to the conversation.

give them	ask him	give him	give her
['gɪvðəm]	['æskəm]	['gɪvəm]	['gɪvər]

A Can I speak to Eric or Cora, please?
B They're not here. Can I give them a message?
A No, that's O.K. Is John there?
B No, he's at work.
A Could you please ask him to call Harold?
B O.K. I'll give him the message.
A Oh, and what about Mary? Is she there?
B No, she's at work, too. Can I give her a message?
A No. I'll call back later.

2. Listen in

Ayako Ono calls Arno's Coffee Shop and talks to Jeff. Read the questions below. Then listen to the phone conversation and answer the questions.

1. What day is George going to call back?
2. What's Ayako's phone number?

3

Nick	Hi, George! Some weather, huh?
George	Yeah, it's terrible . . . but maybe I'll win a trip to Florida.
Nick	Win a trip to Florida?
George	Yeah, I just entered a contest.
Nick	Well, good luck!
George	By the way, your daughter Christine was in the coffee shop today.
Nick	Oh, yeah?
George	She sometimes comes in to talk to Jeff.
Nick	Jeff? Who's Jeff?
George	Well, you know, Jeff Hunt—the boy who works for me in the coffee shop.
Nick	Oh, yeah . . . well, he's a nice guy. Hey, George, are you going to watch the football game tomorrow night?
George	What a question! Of course I am!
Nick	Well, our TV isn't working. Could I . . .
George	Sure! Come over and watch the game with me. Bring Stella too!
Nick	Hey, thanks a lot, George.
George	Any time! Well, listen, I've got to get back.
Nick	Yeah, me too. Say hello to Loretta for me. Tell her to call Stella.
George	O.K. So long! See you tomorrow.

4. Figure it out

True, *False*, or *It doesn't say*?

1. George is going to win a trip to Florida.
2. The weather is terrible in Florida.
3. Jeff and Christine are friends.
4. Nick is Christine's father.
5. George doesn't know Christine.
6. Nick is going to watch the football game with George.
7. Stella wants to watch the football game.

5. Your turn

Loretta answers the phone at Arno's and takes a message for George. The caller's name is Max Shear. Act out a possible conversation between Loretta and Max.

43.

Tips for Success on the Telephone ☎

By Amelia Peretti

You arrive at the airport in another country, but your luggage does not arrive with you. When the airport staff cannot find it, you go unhappily to your hotel room. Now you have to use the telephone for help.

Will someone at the airline help you quickly? Yes, if you are friendly and polite. Good manners are the key to success on the telephone. Here are a few suggestions:

• Speak slowly and pronounce your words clearly. You want the other person to understand you.

• Speak with a smile. People like to hear a pleasant voice.

• Always identify yourself right away. For example, if you make a business call, start with, "Hello, this is Bob Blair. May I speak to Carmen Rivera, please?" For an informal or personal call, you say, "Hi, this is Koji. Is Grace there, please?"

• Be sure to leave a complete message. You can say, "Please ask Ms. Rivera to call me at 555-6821 about our meeting tomorrow" or "Please ask Grace to give me a call about the party on Saturday."

• Finally, always thank the person you speak with. After all, he or she took the time to talk to you. Be sure to use the person's name if you know it. Say, "Thank you very much for your help, Ms. Rivera" or "Thanks a lot, Grace."

These are just a few telephone tips. Try them in *your* next phone call and watch what happens.✐

1. Read the article. Then scan it again and say which of these suggestions it gives.

1. Always give your name when you ask to speak to someone.
2. Speak slowly and clearly.
3. Always leave your phone number.
4. When you thank someone, use the person's name.
5. Always say "hello" and not "hi" when you ask to speak to someone.

2. Do you agree with the tips for success in the article? Which are the most important? Are these tips useful in your country?

Review of units 5-7

1 ▶ **You're a guest at the Blue Water Hotel in Miami. Look at the registration card below. Then copy the form and complete it with personal information.**

The Blue Water Hotel
Miami, Florida

Date_____

_____

Last Name   First Name

_____

Address (Number and Street)

_____

City   State   Zip Code   Country

_____

Home Telephone   Business Telephone

_____

Occupation   Place of Employment

▶ **Exchange registration cards with a partner.**
▶ **Introduce your partner to the class. Give his or her name and occupation.**

2 ▶ **Anna Stasiak is in Miami this week. Complete the paragraphs about her. Fill in the blanks with *in*, *on*, and *at*.**

Anna Stasiak is originally from Krakow, Poland, but she now lives and works _____ London, England. Anna works _____ the Polish Embassy _____ Weymouth Street. She is a translator and interpreter.

Right now, Anna is on vacation _____ Miami. She loves Miami and visits every year. This year she is a guest _____ the Blue Water Hotel _____ Collins Avenue. Anna likes tall buildings and the Blue Water Hotel is very tall. Anna is _____ Room 2234 _____ the twenty-second floor of the hotel.

3 ▶ **Complete the sentences about the staff at the Blue Water Hotel, using the correct singular or plural forms of the nouns in parentheses. Use *a* or *an* if necessary.**

1. Paulo Silva is _*a waiter*_ from Brazil. (waiter)
2. Judy Reinbeck is from Canada, and Maria Lopez is from Mexico. They're both _____ . (waitress)
3. Danielle Michaud is _____ . She's from France. (receptionist)
4. Henri Dubois also speaks French. He's _____ from Haiti. (cook)
5. Mike Ito and Laura Conti are _____ . Mike is from California, and Laura is from New York. (secretary)
6. Bob Schubert is _____ from Miami. (accountant)
7. Lin Wang is _____ . She's from Taiwan. (doctor)

4 ► Imagine you're going to Miami on vacation and you meet another tourist on the flight. Introduce yourself and find out where he or she is from.

A Hi. My name's _____ .
B _____ .
A Are you from Miami?
B _____ . _____ ?
A I'm from _____ .

5 ► Write ten interview questions using the words below to help you. Be sure to use the correct forms of the present tense.

what	brother(s)	wife	parents	Chinese (Spanish, etc.)	speak	go	live	married
where	sister(s)	husband	you	school	have	do	work	

1. _____What do you do ?_____
2. _____
3. _____
4. _____
5. _____
6. _____
7. _____
8. _____
9. _____
10. _____

► Find a student you don't know very well. Interview your partner using the questions above. Write down his or her answers.
► Tell another classmate about your partner.

6 ► Talk about your plans for the weekend with a partner.

A _____ ?
B On Saturday, _____ .
And on Sunday, _____ . What about you?
A _____ .
B Well, have a nice weekend.
A _____ .

7 ► Complete the notes. Fill in the blanks with *me, you, him, her, it, us,* and *them.*

1. Jim,
I'm at the movies.
Mrs. King is going
to call later.
Could you ask
_____ to call
_____ at the
office tomorrow
morning? Thanks.
Alan

2. Emilio:
Mr. Garvey
called. Please
call _____ at
home tonight.

Bill

3. Maria,
How about a
movie? I'll call
_____ tonight.

Alex

4. Taro:
What is Noriko Kitano's
phone number? I don't
have _____ .
Steve

5. Mike,
Aunt Norma and Uncle Frank are in town
this weekend. Please call _____ at 555-
4693.

Mother

6. Bob and Ann,
Please call _____ . It's
very important.
Thanks,
Susan and Martin

8 ► Listen to the telephone calls and complete the two messages.

Marta— _____ Boostani is at the Blue Water Hotel, Room _____ . The phone number is _____ .

Mom

WHILE YOU WERE OUT

FOR Ms. Boostani   **DATE** 6/25/93
FROM Marta _____   **TIME** 2:30 P.M.

Please call Marta _____
at _____ .

9 ► You work in Miami and you're trying to reach Roberto Mendez at the Aztec Export Company in Mexico City. Complete the conversation below.
► Act out the conversation in pairs.

A (*Dials number*) *Rrring, rrring*
B *Buenos días, Aztec. ¿Dígame?*
A _____ ?
B Yes, I do. May I help you?
A _____ ?
B I'm sorry, but he's busy right now. May I give him a message?
A _____ ?
B Could you spell your last name, please?
A _____ .
B And does he have your telephone number?
A _____ .
B Thank you. I'll give him the message.

10A ► Student A follows the instructions below.
Student B follows the instructions on p. A80.

Student A Read the newspaper articles below. Ask your partner questions about Melinda Chan to fill in the blanks. Then answer your partner's questions about Eduardo Sanchez.

The Miami Independent
July 19, 1993

In Miami This Week . . .

MELINDA CHAN TO SING AT ALLIGATOR CLUB

The popular singer Melinda Chan, from _____ , is going to be at the Alligator Club in the Blue Water Hotel on Friday and Saturday, July 23 and 24. She will sing songs from her new hit record *Love Is the Answer*.

Melinda, who is only _____ years old, is popular in many countries around the world. She sings in four languages—Taiwanese, Chinese, _____ , and _____ . "I like languages," she says. "For me, a new language is a new world."

Melinda is rich and famous, but she still lives in a small _____ with her _____ . "My family is very important to me," she says, "and I like my neighbors. I don't want to move."

Melinda likes to travel. This is her first visit to Miami. Next weekend Melinda is going to California to sing in Hollywood. "I'm very excited about that!" she says.

COLOMBIAN COFFEE BUSINESS GOOD IN JAPAN

Eduardo Sanchez, from Colombia, is a very busy international businessman. He visits countries in North and South America, Europe, and Asia and sells coffee. Eduardo is very successful. He is only 38 years old, but he is already a millionaire. "I like my job," he says.

Eduardo speaks Spanish, English, and Japanese. "Japanese is very difficult," he says, "but I try."

Japan is an important country for Eduardo. "The Japanese like coffee and they have many popular coffee houses and cafes in Tokyo, Osaka, Kyoto, and other big cities."

Eduardo lives in Cali, Colombia, the city where he was born, with his wife, Gloria, his son, Carlos, and his daughter, Silvia.

Eduardo is here in Miami this week on vacation. Next week he is going to travel to Italy and Spain.

► Student B follows the instructions below.
 Student A follows the instructions on p. A79.

Student B Read the newspaper articles below. Answer your partner's questions about Melinda Chan. Then ask your partner questions about Eduardo Sanchez to fill in the blanks.

The Miami Independent

July 19, 1993

In Miami This Week . . .

MELINDA CHAN TO SING AT ALLIGATOR CLUB

The popular singer Melinda Chan, from Taipei, Taiwan, is going to be at the Alligator Club in the Blue Water Hotel on Friday and Saturday, July 23 and 24. She will sing songs from her new hit record *Love Is the Answer*.

Melinda, who is only 19 years old, is popular in many countries around the world. She sings in four languages—Taiwanese, Chinese, French, and English. "I like languages," she says. "For me, a new language is a new world."

Melinda is rich and famous, but she still lives in a small apartment with her parents. "My family is very important to me," she says, "and I like my neighbors. I don't want to move."

Melinda likes to travel. This is her first visit to Miami. Next weekend Melinda is going to California to sing in Hollywood. "I'm very excited about that!" she says.

COLOMBIAN COFFEE BUSINESS GOOD IN JAPAN

Eduardo Sanchez, from _____ , is a very busy international _____ . He visits countries in North and South America, Europe, and Asia and sells coffee. Eduardo is very successful. He is only _____ years old, but he is already a millionaire. "I like my job," he says.

Eduardo speaks _____ , _____ , and Japanese. "Japanese is very difficult," he says, "but I try."

Japan is an important country for Eduardo. "The Japanese like coffee and they have many popular coffee houses and cafes in Tokyo, Osaka, Kyoto, and other big cities."

Eduardo lives in _____ , Colombia, the city where he was born, with his _____ , Gloria, his son, Carlos, and his _____ , Silvia.

Eduardo is here in Miami this week on vacation. Next week he is going to travel to _____ and _____ .

 ► Write conversations for these people at Arno's Coffee Shop, using the words in parentheses. Be sure to use the correct forms of the present of *be* and the simple present.

► Act out the conversations with a partner.

1. Maggie Sloane and Nick Pappas meet for the first time.

 Nick (where?)
Maggie (Brooklyn Hospital.)
 Nick (nurse?)
Maggie (lab technician.)

 Nick *Where do you work?*
Maggie *I work at Brooklyn Hospital. . . .*

2. Nick then talks to Maggie's friend Ruth Aguirre.

Nick (what?)
Ruth (biologist.)
Nick (Brooklyn Hospital?)
Ruth (Brooklyn College.)

3. Jeff Hunt wants to call Christine Pappas about some homework. He calls a friend, Gail Gooden, for her phone number.

 Jeff (*Dials number*) *Rrring, rrring*
Gail (Hello?)
 Jeff (there?)
Gail (Gail.)
 Jeff (Jeff.)
Gail (how?)
 Jeff (fine.) (Christine's phone number?)
Gail (555-3217.)

VOCABULARY LIST

This list includes both productive and receptive words introduced in Student Book 1A. Productive words are those which students use actively in interaction exercises. Receptive words are those which appear only in opening conversations, comprehension dialogues, readings, and instructions, and which students need only understand. The letter R appears after each receptive word. Page numbers indicate the first appearance of a word. In the case of productive words, the page indicated is where the word is first used productively. These words generally have been introduced receptively in previous units. This list does not include cardinal numbers, ordinal numbers, countries, languages, or nationalities. These are given in the supplementary vocabulary on pages A85-A86. Also not included are months and days, which can be found on page A58. The following abbreviations are used to indicate parts of speech: V = verb, N = noun, ADJ = adjective, ADV = adverb, PR = pronoun, INTERJ = interjection, 3RD PERS SING = third person singular, PL = plural.

a 36
a cup of 18 R
a few 76 R
a little 63
a lot 36
a lot of 61
abbreviation 30 R
about 5 R
above 26 R
abroad 66 R
according to 54 R
accountant 48
achieve (a goal) 66 R
acquaintance 45 R
across from 34
act out 14 R
activity 72 R
actor 65 R
ad (= advertisement) 29 R
add 25 R
address N 27
address book 27 R
addressed ADJ 30 R
advertisement 29 R
afternoon 70
again 14 R
agree with 76 R
Ah . . . INTERJ 12 R
airline 76 R
airport 76 R
all 30 R
all about it 10 R
all day 60
alone 51
alphabet 7 R
also 40 R
always 20 R
am 4
an 48
and 7
another 7 R
answer N 14 R
answer V 24 R
any 61
Any time! 75 R
Anyway . . . INTERJ 52 R
apartment 35
apologize (for) 17 R
appropriate 50 R
architect 20 R
are 5
Are you crazy or
  something? 38 R

area 40 R
aren't (= are not) 25
around here 51
around the world 44
arrival 22 R
arrive 76 R
article 20 R
artist 57 R
as (work as a waiter) 57 R
ask 7 R
ask for 14 R
association 41 R
at (25 Maple Street) 50
at (Memorial Hospital) 49
at (the corner) 38 R
at night 57 R
at work 14
attraction 40 R
aunt 59
avenue 34
back there 30 R
bad 20 R
bank 34
banker 48
be 5 R
be asleep 20 R
be away 38 R
be buried 40 R
be delayed 22 R
be from 25
be in a hurry 38 R
be interviewed 42 R
be labeled 37 R
be located 34 R
be numbered 37 R
be pronounced 16 R
be related 59 R
be said 58 R
be . . . blocks / miles away.
  38 R
be . . . years old 40 R
beach (go to the beach) 72
beautiful 10 R
begin 60 R
believe 20 R
below 4 R
best (the best =
  SUPERLATIVE of good)
  40 R
between 34
bill 11 R
biology 60
birthdate 58

birthday 58
blank N 20 R
block 50
board N 33 R
board V 56 R
book 72
bookstore 43
borrow 63 R
boss 44
both 77
bother 64 R
boy 64 R
bread 29 R
breakfast 30 R
bring 61 R
brother 59
brother-in-law 28 R
building 37 R
bus stop 45 R
business 41 R
business call 70 R
business phone 63
businessmen (PL of
  businessman) 43
businesswomen (PL of
  businesswoman) 43
busy 67 R
but 30 R
buy 29 R
by the way 75 R
by train 30 R
bye (= good-bye) 26
cafe 79 R
calendar 58 R
call (by a name) 8 R
call (on the telephone)
  12 R
call back 70
Can I . . . ? 71
candy 43
cannot 76 R
carefully 60 R
cemetery 40 R
Certainly. 70
chart 6 R
check 64 R
check V 14 R
cheese 29 R
children (PL of child) 61
choice 66 R

choose 3 R
citizenship 57 R
city 24 R
clarification 63 R
class 26
classmate 4 R
clearly 76 R
close V 33 R
clothing store 36
clue 37 R
coffee 26
coffee house 79 R
coffee shop 8 R
coin 11 R
cold 74 R
colleague 42
come in 8 R
Come on in. 18 R
command N 33 R
common 62 R
company 51
compare 30 R
complete V 5 R
complete ADJ 24 R
conference 42
confirm 16 R
Congratulations! 47 R
construction worker 20 R
contest 74 R
contract 69 R
contraction 4 R
convention center 43
conversation 1 R
cook 48
copy V 63 R
corner 34
correct ADJ 5 R
Could I . . . ? 63
Could you . . . ? 7
country (go to the country)
  72
country 10 R
couple 25 R
coupon 66 R
course 66 R
cousin 59
crazy 38 R
cream 23 R
credit card 11 R
cute 61
dangerous 54 R
date 58
date of birth 63

SUPPLEMENTARY VOCABULARY

SOME OCCUPATIONS

accountant	designer	journalist	psychologist
actor, actress	doctor	laboratory technician	salesperson
architect	doorman	lawyer	sanitation worker
artist	editor	letter carrier	secretary
banker	electrician	mechanic	security guard
barber	engineer	nurse	singer
biologist	factory worker	office worker	taxi driver
bookkeeper	farmer	painter	teacher
bus driver	firefighter	park ranger	telephone operator
carpenter	flight attendant	pharmacist	teller
clerk	florist	photographer	truck driver
counselor	grocer	pilot	waiter, waitress
computer programmer	housekeeper	plumber	word processor
cook	illustrator	professor	writer
dentist	janitor	police officer	veterinarian

SOME NUMBERS

Cardinal		Ordinal	Cardinal		Ordinal
1	one	first	18	eighteen	eighteenth
2	two	second	19	nineteen	nineteenth
3	three	third	20	twenty	twentieth
4	four	fourth	21	twenty-one	twenty-first
5	five	fifth	30	thirty	thirtieth
6	six	sixth	40	forty	fortieth
7	seven	seventh	50	fifty	fiftieth
8	eight	eighth	60	sixty	sixtieth
9	nine	ninth	70	seventy	seventieth
10	ten	tenth	80	eighty	eightieth
11	eleven	eleventh	90	ninety	ninetieth
12	twelve	twelfth	100	one hundred	one hundredth
13	thirteen	thirteenth	101	one hundred and one	one hundred and first
14	fourteen	fourteenth			
15	fifteen	fifteenth	1,000	one thousand	one thousandth
16	sixteen	sixteenth	1,000,000	one million	one millionth
17	seventeen	seventeenth			

SOME FAMILY MEMBERS

M	grandfather	father	son	grandson	brother	husband
F	grandmother	mother	daughter	granddaughter	sister	wife
	grandparents	parents	children	grandchildren		

M	uncle	nephew	cousin	father-in-law	brother-in-law	son-in-law
F	aunt	niece	cousin	mother-in-law	sister-in-law	daughter-in-law

SOME COUNTRIES AND NATIONALITIES

Country	Nationality	Country	Nationality
Algeria	Algerian	Kuwait	Kuwaiti
Argentina	Argentine	Korea	Korean
Afghanistan	Afghan	Laos	Laotian
Australia	Australian	Lebanon	Lebanese
Austria	Austrian	Malaysia	Malaysian
Bolivia	Bolivian	Mexico	Mexican
Brazil	Brazilian	Mongolia	Mongolian
Bulgaria	Bulgarian	Morocco	Moroccan
Canada	Canadian	Nepal	Nepalese
Chad	Chadian	Nicaragua	Nicaraguan
Chile	Chilean	Nigeria	Nigerian
China	Chinese	Norway	Norwegian
Colombia	Colombian	Pakistan	Pakistani
Costa Rica	Costa Rican	Paraguay	Paraguayan
Cuba	Cuban	Peru	Peruvian
Czechoslovakia	Czech	Panama	Panamanian
Ecuador	Ecuadorian	Poland	Polish
Egypt	Egyptian	Portugal	Portuguese
Ethiopa	Ethiopian	Saudi Arabia	Saudi
Finland	Finnish	Spain	Spanish
France	French	Somalia	Somalian
Gambia	Gambian	Sweden	Swedish
Germany	German	Switzerland	Swiss
Guyana	Guyanese	Syria	Syrian
Ghana	Ghanan	Thailand	Thai
Greece	Greek	The Dominican Republic	Dominican
Guatemala	Guatemalan	The Netherlands	Dutch
Haiti	Haitian	The Philippines	Filipino
Honduras	Honduran	The United Kingdom	British
Hungary	Hungarian	The United States of America	American
India	Indian		
Indonesia	Indonesian	Tunisia	Tunisian
Iran	Iranian	Turkey	Turkish
Iraq	Iraqi	Venezuela	Venezuelan
Ireland	Irish	Vietnam	Vietnamese
Israel	Israeli	Zaire	Zairian
Italy	Italian	Zambia	Zambian
Japan	Japanese		
Jordan	Jordanian		
Kenya	Kenyan		

SOME LANGUAGES

Arabic	German	Mongolian	Swedish
Bengali	Greek	Norwegian	Tagalog
Chinese	Hausa	Polish	Tamil
Czech	Hebrew	Portuguese	Thai
Dutch	Hindi	Quechua	Turkish
English	Hungarian	Romanian	Urdu
Farsi	Italian	Russian	Vietnamese
Finnish	Japanese	Spanish	Zulu
French	Korean	Swahili	

P R O N U N C I A T I O N

STRESS AND INTONATION

Affirmative statement: Nice to meet you.

Yes-no question: Hello, is Susan there?

Information questions: Where are you from?

PHONETIC SYMBOLS*

Consonants

[p]	pen, apple
[b]	bank, cabbage
[f]	far, after
[v]	very, have
[k]	coffee, like
[g]	good, again
[l]	letter, mile
[m]	many, name
[n]	never, money
[w]	water, away
[θ]	think, with
[ð]	the, mother
[s]	some, dress
[z]	zero, busy
[ʃ]	shoe, information
[ʒ]	pleasure, measure
[tʃ]	children, teach
[dʒ]	job, age
[r]	right, hurry
[y]	year, million
[h]	he, hat, who
[t]	ten, can't
[d]	dinner, idea

Vowels

[I]	in, visit
[i]	meet, tea
[ɛ]	end, let, any
[æ]	ask, family
[a]	father, hot
[ɔ]	water, long
[ʊ]	could, put
[u]	you, room
[ə]	across, but
[ər]	her, work
[e]	wait, great
[o]	home, go
[aI]	dime, night
[ɔI]	toy, boy
[aʊ]	found, house

*[ə] and [ər] are used in this book for both stressed and unstressed syllables. [y] is used instead of the International Phonetic Alphabet (IPA) [j].

A N S W E R S

Exercise 3, page A5

1. Tom Cruise is an American actor.
2. Janet Jackson is an American singer.
3. Yumi Matsutoya is a Japanese singer/songwriter.
4. Emmanuel is a Mexican singer.

Answers to Exercise 4, page A63

Mucho gusto means "Nice to meet you" in Spanish.
Shukran means "Thank you" in Arabic.
Parakalo means "Please" in Greek.
Obrigado means "Thank you" in Portuguese.
Do svidanye means "Good-bye" in Russian.
Habari gani means "How are you?" in Swahili.
Arigato means "Thank you" in Japanese.
Pen yangai means "How are you?" in Thai.

ACKNOWLEDGMENTS

ILLUSTRATIONS

Storyline illustrations by Anna Veltfort: pages A1, A2-3, A4, A6 (bottom), A8-9, A15, A18-19, A28-29, A38-39, A52-53, A60, A64-65, A74-75; pages A5, A16, A17, A31, A32-33 (except map) A51, A67, A68-69 by Gene Myers; pages A6 (top), A21 (top) (original photo courtesy of Lan Chile), A22, A24 (line drawings), A50 (bottom), A62 by Jim Kinstrey; pages A7, A33 (map), A34 (map), A37 (map), A49, A55, A56-57, A72 by Chris Reed; pages A11 (left), A43 by Don Martinetti; pages A11 (right), A12, A14, A41, A45 by Silvio Redinger; pages A26, A45 (left), A46-47, A50 (top), A59 by Denise Brunkus; pages A36, A63, A70 by Cathy Braffet; page A48 by Arnie Ten.

PHOTOS

Pages A4, A13, A21, A20 (top row and bottom middle), A21, A22-23, A26, A45, A46, A61 by Ken Karp; page A5 (top left) Barry Talesnick/Retna Ltd.; page A5 (top right) Chris Walter/Retna Ltd.; page A5 (bottom left) courtesy of Kirarasha (Kinrara Music Publisher); page A5 (bottom right) © 1990 CBS Records International Inc.; page A10 courtesy Japan National Tourist Organization; page A20 (bottom left) Ed Lettau/Photo Researchers; page A54 (top left) Laima Druskis; page A54 (top right) City of New York Department of Sanitation; page A54 (middle left) Laima Druskis; page A54 (middle right) Laima Druskis, page A54 (bottom left) Laima Druskis; page A66 (middle) courtesy British Tourist Authority.

REALIA

Pages A10, A16, A20, A24 (map), A27, A30, A40, A42, A43, A44, A54, A55, A56, A57, A63, A66, A70, A71, A73, A76 by Roberto de Vicq; pages A22, A36, A41, A77, A78, A79, A80 by Deborah Brennan.

REVIEWERS AND CONSULTANTS

Regents/Prentice Hall would like to thank the following long-time users of *Spectrum*, whose insights and suggestions have helped to shape the content and format of the new edition: Motofumi Aramaki, *Sony Language Laboratory*, Tokyo, Japan; *Associacão Cultural Brasil-Estados Unidos (ACBEU)*, Salvador-Bahia, Brazil; *AUA Language Center*, Bangkok, Thailand, Thomas J. Kral and faculty; Pedro I. Cohen, Professor Emeritus of English, Linguistics, and Education, *Universidad de Panamá*; *ELSI Taiwan Language Schools*, Taipei, Taiwan, Kenneth Hou and faculty; James Hale, *Sundai ELS*, Tokyo, Japan; *Impact*, Santiago, Chile; *Instituto Brasil-Estados Unidos (IBEU)*, Rio de Janeiro, Brazil; *Instituto Brasil-Estados Unidos No Ceará (IBEU-CE)*, Fortaleza, Brazil; *Instituto Chileno Norteamericano de Cultura*, Santiago, Chile; *Instituto Cultural Argentino Norteamericano (ICANA)*, Buenos Aires, Argentina; Christopher M. Knott, *Chris English Masters Schools*, Kyoto, Japan; *The Language Training and Testing Center*, Taipei, Taiwan, Anthony Y. T. Wu and faculty; *Lutheran Language Institute*, Tokyo, Japan; *Network Cultura, Ensino e Livraria Ltda*, São Paulo, Brazil; *Seven Language and Culture*, São Paulo, Brazil.